RUSSELL GRANT'S
1993 HOROSCOPES

Books by Russell Grant

Your Love Signs
Your Sun Signs
Dream Dictionary
1993 Horoscopes

RUSSELL GRANT'S

1993 HOROSCOPES

LEO

24 July-23 August

Virgin

First published in Great Britain in 1992 by
Virgin Books
an imprint of Virgin Publishing Ltd
338 Ladbroke Grove
London W10 5AH

ISBN 0 86369 564 7

A catalogue record for this title is available from the British Library

Illustrations by Maggie Kneen

Typeset by Phoenix Photosetting, Chatham, Kent.
Printed in Great Britain by
Cox & Wyman Ltd, Reading, Berks.

CONTENTS

INTRODUCTION

Welcome to the latest edition of my astrological almanac, full of information about the starry trends coming your way in nectarine 1993!

If you've been wondering what the New Year has in store for you, then you need look no further than the packed pages of this book, for it contains all you need to know for an enjoyable, enterprising and successful annum. If you're a regular reader of my columns and books, then you'll know by now that astrology is all about forecasting the possible pitfalls, problems and possibilities indicated by the planets' positions and relationships in the heavens. It can't determine your destiny, because only you can do that by exercising your free will, but what it can do is point out all the good and bad vibes that are surrounding you. Then you can cash in on every opportunity that comes your way, or turn nasty or negative situations to your advantage by being prepared for them in advance. And there's a special section outlining your amorous, pecuniary and professional prospects over the coming year. Let's face it, we can all be wise after the event, but wouldn't it be better to be wise beforehand?

How energetic and enterprising are you? Do you jump out of bed with a spring in your step, look to the future and ambitiously aim straight for the top? Or do you prefer to take a back seat and let other folk beat you to the winning post? It's all to do with the sign

1

that martial Mars occupied when you were born, so turn to the first half of this book if you want to know more and discover just how dynamic you can be.

They say that love makes the world go round, but how do you feel about all things romantic? If you want to make the most of your *affaires de coeur* then you need to follow the planetary progress of voluptuous Venus as she sashays her way through the celestial sky during nectarine 1993. Plot her path through your horoscope with my simple chart and you'll be all set to get the most out of love, leisure and pleasure in the annum ahead.

Wondering why a relationship's reached rock bottom, or want to know how you'll fare with someone you've just met? Then look no further than my chapters on the twelve Sun signs, and also my relationship guide, to learn everything you need to know about getting on with others. Want to know your lucky number, day of the week or birthstone? Then turn to my chart giving the traditions of astrology, and start reading!

If you're always wondering where to go on holiday, then why not let the stars give you a few hints? Turn to my travel guide to see which towns, cities and countries are ideal for your Sun sign. You could be in for a big surprise!

Once you've read all that, plus my day-by-day forecasts, you'll be all set for a propitious, providential and positive new year. Enjoy yourself!

RUSSELL'S GUIDE TO THE SUN SIGNS

ARIES – 21 MARCH–20 APRIL

Me, me, me, me! No, it's not an opera singer practising the scales, but the Arien catch-phrase. This is the first sign of the zodiac, and Ariens like everyone to remember that. (First come, first served, is the Martian motto.) And because this is such a fun-loving, frisky sign, Ariens can get away with it.

The positive side of Aries is like a scene from *The African Queen*, in which our intrepid explorers boldly go where only crocodiles have gone before. Ariens are active, alive, awake (usually), assertive and adventurous, hacking their way through the undergrowth of life like Marlon Brando in a steamy movie. (Yes, he's an Arien!) But they can take this exuberance to extremes. (They can take a lot of things to extremes!) Ariens can step out, putting their best feet forward (all four of them – well, they are animals!) and sinking up to their best end of necks in trouble.

Luscious Libra is the polar sign of assertive Aries, and these signs have a lot to learn from each other. Librans always put others first, which is something Ariens find almost impossible to do. In fact, a relationship between these two is their idea of heaven, because they both think about the Arien. (And of course, after 'Me', the Ram's favourite word is 'Ewe'!)

Sometimes, this can cause a contretemps in the course of true

3

love. Male Ariens may forget about the wife and six kids at home and gad about like a bachelor gay with a collection of conquests. Arien women may throw their weight about too, demanding new dresses and wanting to be taken to the best restaurants, even when their men haven't got two halfpennies to rub together.

Aries is ruled by Mars, the planet that gives them that gorgeous get-up-and-go, that delicious drive and determination. (As long as they're not determinedly driving all over delicious *you*!) Mighty Mars rules Scorpio, too, when he shares the limelight with powerful Pluto. Then he can make Scorpios furtive and underhand, but when he's in open Aries, it's a very different story. Ariens can be so candid and frank that it's an excruciating experience to hear them. You can meet your Martian mate for a meal, and swan in, looking sensational. (Or so you think, you poor dear.) The Arien will take one look at you and say 'That frock makes you look fatter than ever.' (How can you then say that you've just lost two stone – and a pal in the process!)

There's something rather ingenuous about Aries. Because this is the first sign of the zodiac, Rams represent the babies of the celestial sky. Sometimes they're so naive and innocent it's astounding, and they'll dash off and do or say something really reckless. (Or just plain potty!) They can also have terrible temper tantrums, like a tirading toddler, and shout and scream till they're blue in the face. Assertive Ariens are so determined to get what they want that they'll let nothing stand in their way. They'll go on until it kills them.

Every sign has its own song, and the Arien's aria must be 'Let's Get Physical'. (Take that in any way you like. After all, they will!) Rams are imbued with enough physical energy to fill a whole football team (and a stand of supporters!). But, like children, they have to find positive pursuits in which to burn it all off. Ariens are full of fire, fun, vivacity, verve and virility. (Quite a captivating concoction, which can really go to your head!) But they can fritter away their fantastic physical fitness, and instead of having an active social, sports or sex life, turn to violence and vandalism. (Even the meekest and mildest mutton will show a strong side sometimes, and may bop you on the bonce for no apparent reason.) Some of these Martians can be all brawn and no brain, thinking with their fists – or any other part of the anatomy that springs to mind! (Ariens have powerful passions and strong sex drives!)

Ariens are like medieval knights, arrayed in armour and jousting for superiority. Their Fiery natures make them compulsively competitive, and determined to do battle. They have *got* to come first. Rams, lambs and sheep hate losing, whether at Ludo, life or love. (They'll just throw the dice for a six and start again.) When they see success slipping away, they'll fight tooth and claw, frightening off folk in their flocks. Watch out, watch out, there's a Ram about!

TAURUS – 21 APRIL–21 MAY

Taureans are very easy creatures to understand. They have very basic needs: male Bulls love grub and girls, and females of this sign adore food and fellas. Simple, isn't it?

Being the first of the Earth signs, Taurus symbolises rich, rolling fields of very dark brown earth waiting to be cultivated. The Sun sits in the sign of Taurus at Maytime, and so Taurus is linked with the ritual of May Day, the maypole, young maidens, and earthy, pagan customs and folklore.

Taureans are governed by their love of sensuality in all its forms, and some of them can go a mite mad and overindulge themselves, whether it's with sex or a simmering stew with delicious dumplings.

A lot of Taureans have very expressive, often deep-set eyes, that can put across their message better than a million Gemini words. I know one normally sensible, sane Capricorn girl who was reduced to a gibbering wreck when one of these Bulls looked at her across a crowded room. He didn't have to say a word – his eyes did all the talking. (I'd wondered why she suddenly blushed like a beetroot.)

Bulls hate change. They need to know that tomorrow will be the same as today, and that the day after tomorrow will be the same as a week next Wednesday. This is not a sign that is moved by challenge, but Bulls can show tremendous endeavour, patience, persistence and resoluteness.

I have many Taurean chums, and what I absolutely adore about them is that when you go to visit them, you will have barely opened the garden gate before they've offered you a cuppa and asked you if you've eaten. (Say no.) They can be wonderfully warm and welcoming, really making you feel at home, and wondering what they can give you that is theirs. (More stew?)

Ownership is very important to Taureans. Seeing a room full of furniture they've paid for, or a freezer full of food, makes them feel secure. However, negative Taureans can be so possessive and narrow-minded that they can class wives, husbands, kids and pets in the same category as the couch and the cooker and feel that they own them lock, stock and barrel.

To give you an idea of the good and bad sides of the Bull, a country said to be ruled by Taurus is the Emerald Isle. Think of the simple, relaxed way of life there, those glorious greens and beautiful browns of the Irish countryside; then think of the widespread bigotry over religion with both sides refusing to compromise, and you have Taurus at its worst.

In fact, one description of Taurus that you will hear time and time again is 'stubborn as a mule'. Certainly, Taurus is a Fixed sign, and Taureans can be as hard to shift as a sack of soggy cement, but I do think this so-called stubbornness is a wee bit overemphasised. Of course, there is a diabolical dose of dogged determination in the Taurean character, but these Bulls are not always as obstinate and obtuse as they are portrayed. In fact, if used positively, this steadfast streak can lead to persistence and determination. On the negative side, it can lead to rumbustious rows because of the Taurean's intransigence and inability to see another person's point of view.

But make no mistake. If used in the right way, fixity can be a wonderful thing. If Bulls want something slightly out of reach, they will put their heads down and charge (slowly) straight for it, eventually achieving their goal, even if it kills them in the process!

As you might expect from a sign that symbolises the countryside, often Taureans aren't very happy in the city – unlike Air or Fire signs, who like hustle and bustle. Taureans, on the other hand, need to live in a place where they can commune with nature, feeling the ground beneath their feet and seeing the sky above their heads. Bulls will be at their best in a verdant village, or a comfy crofter's cottage. City Bulls will have stacks of window boxes crammed with leafy flora, to give them that 'at home' feeling. Bulls' abodes will be warm and welcoming, unless they are going through a desperate disruption or change in their relationships.

Taureans rarely do anything quickly, choosing to take their time. If they're negative, they may prefer to pretend that their position, passionwise, is pootchy, when even the fly on the wall can see that it isn't. Eventually the world will crumble around their ears, when their amour ambles off with another. Everyone except the Bull will have seen exactly what was happening, and not be outraged at the outcome.

Taureans find it especially difficult to accept change in their emotional relationships, because fidelity and loyalty are paramount to them. But whether a Taurean likes it or not (probably not), changes of some sort or another will be inevitable in their lives, and the sooner they get used to the idea the better. The more they can make themselves cope with change, the less heartache they will have in the long run. I know many Taureans who have resisted an upheaval that was inevitable, and gone through hell and high water as a result.

Venus rules Taurus and Libra, endowing both signs with a love of beauty and a need for harmony, although they seek these ideals in different ways. When ruling Libra, Venus is lighter and more sanguine, but she's much deeper and richer in Taurus. Librans love Rodgers and Hammerstein, while Taureans will opt for opera. They love the beauty of flowers, the earth and all the good things in life, and with their classical, traditional outlook, can teach a lot of the more restless signs quite a lesson or two. So don't fall into the trap of thinking Taureans are simply bull-headed. They can be obstinate, though they would call it being strong-minded!

GEMINI – 22 MAY–21 JUNE

If you want to know how a Gemini ticks, sidle up to the one you're trying to puzzle out, start up a chatette, and then listen very carefully. Above the twinkling tones of the Twin twittering on, you may hear a weird whirring, combined with a couple of clicks. Yes? Well, congratulations, my dears, you have just heard the Gemini brain cells in action. And they are what make every Gemini tick.

The more astute Twins will actually admit to being aware of their Mercurial minds working. They can *feel* themselves thinking. Just imagine all those neurons neoning away inside their noddles. Geminis think so quickly that they leave some of the other signs standing. Everything they see and hear will pass through that brilliant brainbox and be stored away for future reference in the Geminian filing system.

If you're meeting a Gemini for the first time, you'll notice how nervously and quickly he or she moves. Even if the Twin is sitting talking to you, his or her eyes will be taking in everything in the room, and everything about you. Even the egg stain on your tie and the fascinating fact that you're wearing odd socks!

Geminis have a very low boredom threshold, and you'll soon know if you've made them cross it. Their peepers will be poring all over the place and rarely popping back to you. (Apart from your egg stain, of course, because they'll be dying to ask you if it was boiled or fried.) Their fingers will begin to tap out tunes on the table, their feet will jiggle up and down, and they will become fantastically fidgety. This is a danger sign, and unless you can suddenly turn the conversation on to a different, more scintillating subject, to ignite their interest again, you may as well give up and go home. Otherwise you'll be written off as being too boring to bother with.

All Geminis have an elfin appearance, and look like potential pixies. It's rare for them to look like hobgoblins, because this is a very attractive sign, both mentally and physically. The typical Twin – male or female – is incredibly pretty in a boyish way, with alert, shining eyes and fine features.

Most Twins have a very fast way of talking, and may even start to stammer when excited. That may sound strange when you consider that Geminis are so glib and garrulous, and graced with the gift of the gab, but actually sometimes their minds move faster than their mouths, and you get a right old scramble coming out! Geminis love puns because it means they can play about with their favourite toys – words.

Every sign has its good and bad side, and Gemini is no exception. Positively, Geminis are incredibly lively, witty people, extremely articulate and natural communicators. But the reverse of that is the Twin who uses communications in the wrong way, and tells terrible lies (like Matilda's, they make one gasp and stretch one's eyes). Some Geminis like to bend the truth into real reef knots: they can be real Uri Gellers with words.

A lot of Geminis say to me, 'Oh, I'm two-faced, because I'm a Twin,' but I think they've got it wrong. The popular myth is that all Geminis are raving schizophrenics, or Jekyll and Hyde characters, being sweet as sugar one minute and ravening beasties the next. You have to look at Gemini's ruling planet, Mercury, to work this out. As it spins about the solar system, one side of it is always in darkness, and the other is always light. And it's the same with the Twins. When we talk of dark and light in a personality, we can mean a true schizophrenic, with two personalities in one mind, or simply someone, like a Gemini, who experiences a tremendous variety of emotions within *one* personality. Geminis can certainly have extremes of character, and on one level be alert, bright, chatty and chirpy, and on another, be so depressed they can't even find the words to describe how miserable they are.

Very often, Geminis can be desperately disappointed with the world. It can be such a dull place, full of such dreary people that Twins have to invent their own, brighter world to cheer themselves up. Geminian memories of events are always a slightly different version of what really happened!

If you understand this it'll help you to appreciate the Twins you know better. You should even feel a bit sorry for them, if you think about it. People who live in their heads that much are bound to be lonely, at least some of the time.

CANCER – 22 JUNE–23 JULY

Cuddle and caress a Cancerian you know, today! Crabs need to feel safe and secure, and to know that they are adored and amoured.

This is the sign of Moons and Junes – literally! Leo is led by the Sun, but Cancer is ruled by the other leading light of the zodiac, the Moon. Throughout history and legend, the Moon has always represented motherhood, and she rules the tides, menstruation, and everything else associated with the 28-day cycle. (No, it's not a new form of transport!) The Moon is the peaceful, passive, defensive drive within us, and in the natal chart she shows our maternal instincts, habits and childhoods, and whether we love or loathe our mums.

Generally speaking, Cancerians are ultra-protective, and that can mean they protect themselves as well as others. (Well, aren't crabs encased in shells?) A very good friend of mine says that if you think of a rocker, clad in chain mail and leather, looking fearfully ferocious, then try to imagine taking all that chain mail off, you'll find a very ordinary person underneath. And you can say exactly the same thing about Cancer the Crab. There they are, with that solid shell, that concrete coating, waving their pincers about provocatively, and pretending to be pugnacious. But get out the crab cracker and you have the main ingredient for a rather nice crab sandwich – sweet and soft! (Slap two slices of brown bread around them, quick!)

When you first meet a Cancerian, you will sense a hardness, tetchiness, and moodiness, as Crabs are always on the defensive! These are the folk who rush into the room and slap you round the face, just in case you're going to be nasty!

On a positive level, this is a devoted sign. Crabs have a fierce family feeling, can get quite clannish, and put their kith and kin at the centre of their universes.

Many Cancerian men tie the nuptial knot, but can't untangle the apron strings that bind them to their mums and dads. This can cause fantastic flare-ups within their marriages, because their wives feel upstaged by their mothers-in-law. And lots of Cancerian women spend almost all their weekends with their parents in the bosom (what a nice Cancerian word!) of their families, even when they've got a husband and six kids at home. (Maybe that's why!)

Crabs can remember what they had for breakfast on their second birthdays, but they can also remember when you last let them down. They will hurl back past slights, which happened many moons before, in the middle of a row. They also like to live in the past (ever seen a Crab in a crinoline?), and they're very traditional, and tremendous collectors of bits and bobs, especially if they are full of memories. (They call them mementoes. Other people call them tat.) And they hoard letters like mad! (A true Crab will have kept all the letters he or she has ever received from the age of six months onwards.)

You see, they hate to throw things away. (Just in case they come in handy.) A Cancerian friend of mine once went whizzing off to a jumble sale at eleven in the morning loaded with the memorabilia (another good Cancerian word) she was chucking out. At half past three she bought the lot back for ten bob. She couldn't bear to part with a single sock!

Being a Water sign, and ruled by the Moon, Crabs are powerfully psychic, and they will have incredibly intuitive instincts. (When they say they're tuning in, they're not talking about the radio!) Crowds of Cancerians can walk into a room and instantly pick up an atmosphere. (And I don't mean the sultry scent of Saturday's supper – sprouts and stew – either.) Their superb sensitivity also means they can be hurt far too easily, and often over nothing at all. Some of them are hypersensitive, and should realise that when they are told something, it's not always meant as a criticism, or an out-and-out rejection.

Cancerians should try to toughen their soft skins which sit beneath their shells, and not harbour hurts or supposed slights. When they do take umbrage, they become changeable and crabby, mean, moody, huffy and hostile, and almost unapproachable at times. They should use their highly-developed instincts in a positive manner, and trust them and live by them. (Very intense Crabs will tune into their teapots, saying at about four in the afternoon, 'I feel I should put the kettle on.' If you're there, try saying you can sense a custard cream hovering in the biscuit tin.)

Security is of vital importance to Cancerians; often if they feel down and depressed, and are doddering about in the doldrums, it's because they don't have a real base to go home to. They need the emotional security of having their own four walls about them, whereas Taureans need nests for material security.

If you're married to a Cancerian, or have a chum who's a Crab, you have to behave like a cuckoo clock, and at every half hour pop your head round the door and say 'I love you!' (You must mean it, though.) Then they'll feel safe and secure. (Go on, give 'em a kiss!) They can be so gruff that they take you by surprise sometimes. So, if you know a Cancerian who is being crabby, just remember the rocker with the chain mail. (If you're a Bull, you'll remember the crab sandwich!) Underneath that hard shell shimmers a heart of pure gold, which is just waiting to melt as the first words of love cascade from your lips!

Now, of course, there are some cantankerous, cross and cranky Crabs about. They'll be mean and moody, and will scowl like scallops. They'll click away with their pincers, sounding like a couple of castanets on a package holiday, but they will still be soft and sweet underneath.

Cancerians really do need to be needed, and know that they're loved. Otherwise, they can't function fully. Remember this is the polar sign of Capricorn, and most Goats are frightened of rejection. Crabs can be just the same. If they do have particularly firm filial feelings, especially for a matriarchal mum, they'll prefer to hide at home than go out into the big wide world and face whatever it may have to offer them. And when they do scuttle out from under a rock to test the waters of life, if they're used and abused, they'll sound a furious fandango with their perpetually pirouetting pincers, and then rush back to the boulder as fast as their pins can propel them.

Babies are a must for this sign. Whereas procreation is important for Leos, who love children and like to be proud of their own cubs, with Cancer it is much deeper, and more a case of carrying on the family name. Cynthia Crab. Cyril Crab . . .

LEO – 24 JULY–23 AUGUST

Inside every Leo is a king or queen waiting to jump out. (In a little Leo it'll be a prince or princess.) But whatever the rank, Leos do like to wear the crown, hold the sceptre, and be in charge. It's a Leo who will lead a little old lady across the road, even when she doesn't want to go! (You try arguing with a Lion halfway across a zebra crossing!)

Leo's aren't going to like this, but what makes many of them tick is acres of applause. They like to be the centre of attention and know that their public – whether it's 5000 fans or the boy next door – appreciates them.

There are some very colourful Leos around, but there are some very grey ones too. Think of a Leo, and you'll see someone blond and blue-eyed, with a magnificent mane of hair. The men always look like Apollo, who is associated with this sunny sign. And the women are stunningly striking, and have long golden tresses (even if they are out of a bottle!), which shimmer every time they toss their heads in a majestic manner. However, there's another sort, too. This breed look a little like moles, not lions at all, with black barnets, piggy peepers and a rather shifty air! It's very hard to believe that they belong to this splendid sign, but they do!

But whatever they look like, there's no doubt that positive Leos will offer you the earth and give you their hearts. (Gold-plated ones, of course.) There is a gorgeous grandiosity about Leos, but sometimes they can be all mouth. It's only when it's too late that you realise the Lion was just out to impress you.

There was a Lion I used to know, who would offer everyone the earth. He made you feel there was nothing he wouldn't do for you, and promises, offers and assurances flew from his mouth like bees from a hive. The trouble was that those bees never made any honey! It was all hot air, and that's very disappointing indeed from a Lion.

You must never forget (as if the Lions would let you!) that Leo is ruled by the Sun, the centre of the solar system. This star controls almost everything and we'd die without the heat from its rays. So, a lot of Leos can live their lives with a Sun complex. The modest wee beasts feel that as the Sun is the centre of the solar system, so they are centre of the human race!

As a result, of course, they expect people to put down the red carpet for them. Everything has to be done in a stately, stylish way, as if entertaining royalty. When a Leo comes to tea, he or she won't want to be fobbed off with just one fairy cake, but will demand a three-tiered Victoria sponge. This is a regal, dignified and imperial sign, and the Leo will be either an Emperor Nero or Good Queen Bess. But whatever part he or she is playing, it has to be one that doesn't go unnoticed. Leos don't like to be just one of the crowd, like an extra in a scene from *Gone With the Wind*. They want to be Rhett Butler or Scarlett O'Hara. (Lions with strong Cancerian links will want to play Tara, the O'Hara home!)

In astrology, the Sun is our creative core, so Leo is said to be the most creative of the signs. Leos may portray this by playing Annie in *Annie Get Your Gun* at the local amateur dramatic society or by painting their self-portraits on a 40-foot canvas. If they can't be creative themselves in an active way, they'll do it passively, taking off to the theatre or burying themselves in a book. (Why not start with this one?)

Make no mistake, Leo is the sign of the Hollywood musical extravaganza. It may be a bit brash, but it'll have a massive orchestra, and you'll be spellbound by the majesty of it all. And that's what Leos love most. Neptune was tripping the light fantastic through Leo during the great age of Hollywood musicals, which is why they were so lavish. And believe it or not, lots of film producers and directors are Leos – Sam Goldwyn, Alfred Hitchcock, Busby Berkeley and Cecil B. De Mille were all born under this splendid sign of the silver screen. (Leos certainly know how to do things in style.)

There's a fantastic feeling of leisure and pleasure about this sign. Leos love enjoying themselves. (And that's not as obvious as it sounds. Virgos and Capricorns sometimes feel guilty when they have a good knees-up.) They also adore being seen with the right people. (Up-market Leos will be the people the other Leos want to be seen with!)

What makes most Leos tick, though, is very simple. It's the biggest heart imaginable – a sort of titanic ticker. Positive Lions can be wonderfully warm and lastingly loving. And as if that weren't enough, they have a rich sense of humour running through them that will surround you and make you feel safe and secure.

Some Leos aren't lovable Lions at all, but are cheetahs, literally. This sneaky side of the sign comes from the Leonine lust for power. These crafty cats won't have the personality or warmth of the positive Leo, so will have to achieve their ambitions through underhand acts. Don't expect all Leos to want to be centre-stage, because some of them will prefer to wait in the wings, looking on. But most Leos love the limelight, and are happier playing the main man or leading lady. (They may even stick gold stars on their bedroom doors at home.) These Leos aren't concerned with the chorus; they want the bright lights and all that goes with them. Their love of luxury means they can look and dress the part to perfection. But very often they'll behave abominably, and treat everyone as if they were their servants. Don't let a Lion make you his or her skivvy!

Just because a Leo chooses *not* to come on like a Hollywood hotchpotch of Mae West, Cleopatra (don't let her get the needle), and Napoleon Bonaparte, doesn't mean he or she is negative. Sometimes, it's quite the reverse! All you need is a peek at a pirouetting and preening prima donna to see what produces a positive Leo. Some Lions will convey their creative concerto in a quieter, more controlled way. (A Moonlight Sonata rather than an 1812 Overture!) But a positive pussycat will always be the sunshine of your life.

VIRGO – 24 AUGUST–23 SEPTEMBER

Now, before we go any further, think about the Virgos you know. (They're the ones with the neat hairdos and shiny shoes, who make you feel as if you've just been dragged through a hedge backwards.) One of the wonderful things about Virgos is their tremendous talent for organising everything under the sun – starting with themselves. And they really come into their own when they can organise others as well, whether as a cleaning lady or as Home Secretary.

Vestal Virgos of all shapes and sizes are only too pleased to give you a helping hand; their Mercurial motto is 'Service with a smile'. What's more, they really live up to it. You can phone your friend when you're in a fix, and the Virgo will zoom round in ten seconds flat, looking as neat as a new pin. (How do they do it?) If you're feeling as if you've been slung on the scrapheap of life, a Virgo will interrupt your tale of woe with a hundred handy hints and then try to find you another job.

The next thing to remember about this sign is their ceaseless search for perfection. And because they're ruled by Mercury, the planet of the mind and communication, they do this analytically. Geminis spend a lot of time thinking too, but in a swifter, more superficial way. Mercury is more practical in Virgo, restrained by the Earthy element of this sign. This quest for all things perfect means that Virgos don't suffer fools gladly; they like everything to be of the best, both materially and mentally. Sometimes this can go too far, and a Virgo will become fussy and finicky to a fanatical degree. These folk can pick holes in everything, because nothing matches up to their ideals. (But take heart, because the faults they most often find are within themselves.)

Before you've spent five minutes with vestal Virgos you'll have noticed they're naturally neat, and like things to be spick and span, and in apple-pie order. This is the sign of cleanliness, both inner and outer. With most Virgos, this means they just keep everything hunky-dory, but others can go overboard. You'd think they had disinfectant swirling through their systems, they're so obsessed about their health. (A vulnerable Virgoan will moan 'If health is wealth, then I'm broke.')

Now, you may think this sounds a bit much, and that your Virgo pals aren't like that. But they are, even if it's just in a weensy way. Next time you meet a Mercurial mate, listen carefully to the conversation. There'll be at least one reference to keeping clean or tidy, I promise, or you'll hear about their health and hygiene. (This is the sign of hypochondria!) Still not convinced? Well, next time you have a chat in a café with your chum, do a bit of brow-clutching, or seize your stomach and sigh. Say you have a headache, or that you'd better steer clear of the sausage surprise, in case it gives you one later. Your Virgo will come over all concerned, burrow into a bag or briefcase, and produce just the pill guaranteed to get you going again. (They're *that* well organised!)

When it comes to keeping their surroundings sparkling, Virgos beat everyone dusters down. If they visit you, they'll even do your tidying up, not even noticing what they're doing. There was a Virgo girl at school who was invited to more parties then all the debs in Devon, because her idea of a good time was frolicking with the

Fairy Liquid in the kitchen. Put your shandy down for a second and she'd have whizzed in and whisked it away, then given the glass a good going-over in the suds in the sink. (Invite a few Virgos to your next knees-up, and you won't even have to clear away a cup – it'll all be done for you! But you've got to pick the right sort, because some of them are unutterably untidy.)

Because Virgos are usually tidy-minded and orderly, they can be somewhat sceptical and suspicious of anything they don't under-stand. For them, seeing is believing: they're innately inquisitive, and like to find things out for themselves. That means it's hard to pull the wool over their eyes, because they can see straight through any fast-talking. Anyone who's a fly-by-night won't stand a chance once those Mercurial minds get moving.

Virgos who make the most of their mental mastery and organis-ational ability can go a long way at work. (And I don't mean they make lovely long-distance lorry drivers, either!) But you might not hear about that almost certain success. Virgos are very modest, and hate blowing their own trumpets. Even when they win accolades and awards they'll prefer to keep quiet.

Unfortunately, Virgos sometimes carry this ravishing reticence into other areas of their lives. Not only will they be coy profession-ally, but they'll be retiring romantically, too. Their heads usually rule their hearts and Virgos can be quite cool, undemonstrative and unemotional. One Virgo relative of mine married purely for tax reasons.

This is definitely a sign that finds it hard to slow down, and Mercury makes Virgos move about like maniacs – busy bees! They can have dreadful difficulties relaxing, and will always find some-thing to do, even if it's the dusting – for the third time in a morning. Which reminds me. I was chatting to a Mercurial male one day, and we were discussing what he'd done during Christmas. He said his girlfriend had gone to Glasgow, and left him at home. Did he mind? 'Oh no!' he grinned. 'It meant I could tidy up my flat. And I got the tops of the plugs clean. It was wonderful!' Obviously he got thirteen amps of joy from Santa that Christmas!

LIBRA – 24 SEPTEMBER–23 OCTOBER

Sugar and spice and all things nice – that's what Librans are made of. Even if you get the rare one made from puppy-dogs' tails, you can bet they'll be pretty pooches and handsome hounds. So it may come as a shock to you that this sweet, sublime sign is the iron hand in the velvet glove. 'What? Our Ethel?' I can hear you saying, but read on, my dears. Libra is a Cardinal Air sign, which means that Librans know what they want, and usually have the mental mastery to be able to get it. I mean, look at Margaret Thatcher!

Libra's ruling planet is Venus, which makes subjects of this sign courteous, charming, cheerful, caring, caressable and captivatingly cuddly. Make no mistake, loquacious Librans can charm the birdies right out of the trees when they want to. (And scintillate the squirrels while they're about it.) But if you look closely, they usually have an aim for all that charm and diplomacy.

Take a woman who has the Sun, Moon, Mars and Jupiter all in luscious Libra. (Gosh!) One day she discovered that a near-neighbour didn't give two hoots about her so she moved heaven and earth until she did, but she killed her with kindness in the process! (And piqued all her pals, who felt ignored.)

The trouble is that Librans like to be liked. In fact, they can't bear to believe that someone can't stand them. Venus can bestow beauteous bounty on her boys and girls, but sometimes she can make them too sweet for words. Even when a Libran is at his or her sugariest and sickliest, you must work out what's behind it all. Librans are assertive, ambitious and go-ahead. So they always have an end in sight. (*Votre derrière*, dear.) It could be to keep the peace (incredibly important to Librans), or to get a new job, but it will be something. Of the other Cardinal signs, Ariens will tramp through the rest of the zodiac, Cancerians will drown everyone in tears, and Capricorns will lumber along like a ten-ton tank. But Librans try to get what they want with a smile. (And they usually succeed.)

This is the sign of nuptial bliss, of partnerships of all persuasions, both in business and in love. (Committed relationships of one sort or another loom large in a Libran life.) And so it's the sign of enemies, too. After all, you can have a rapport with a rival just as much as you'll have an affinity with an amourette. The strength of the emotion is the same. Although the Libran motto is 'Peace at all costs', you mustn't forget the razor's edge between love and hate.

The polar sign of Libra is Aries, and these two can have a wonderful relationship, because they balance each other beauti-fully. (And remember that though Librans, being the sign of the Scales, are always trying to achieve perfect harmony in their lives, their own set of scales can go up and down like yo-yos.) The archetypal Arien-Libran relationship is the Tarzan and Jane jamboree. There's Arien Tarzan swinging through the shrubbery, leaping about in a little loincloth, while Libran Jane stays at home being perky and pretty, probably with a little dishcloth. (Wearing it, of course, in a lovely shade of pink.) The Libran's keyword is 'You', whereas Ariens say '*Me!*'. Librans can think too much of their partners and pals, to their own detriment, and can stride off through sleet and snow to minister to a mate who's ill. Some of them can be too selfless for words, although they may still be doing it for a reason – to be liked and loved!

Librans should stop being so concerned with the welfare of their loved ones, and think of themselves sometimes instead. In astrology, every sign has a positive and a negative side, and if you go to extremes in either direction it can be terrible.

This is the sign of puffy pink clouds, baby-blue angora wool and pink-and-white icing. You see, Libra is a very pretty sign indeed. It's not as fantastical and fairy-tale as the Fish, because Librans have more of a sense of reality. Nevertheless, the Libran quest is very much for beauty, and with this love for all things bright and beautiful, Librans can't cope with anything coarse, callous or crude.

The trouble with Librans is that they can be irritatingly indecisive; you can go grey while waiting for them to make up their minds about whether to feast on a fairy cake or have a blow-out on bangers and mash. (In the end you want to bash them over the bonce with the frying pan.) That may be why they're so considerate, and always ask you what *you* want to do, what *you* want to eat – because they know they haven't the foggiest idea. (Although lots of them *do* know, and try to coerce you into choosing their choice.)

They also like to keep everything fair and square, and if they feel they've been wronged, they'll fight like Aries or be as stubborn as the most intransigent Taurean to prove they're in the right. Justice must be seen to be done – in the Libran's eyes, at least. (Negative Librans will get their sense of justice a mite mixed up.) But even positive Librans will tamper with the balance they find in their lives, on their oh-so-sensitive scales, and wonder if they've got it right. ('On the other hand,' they'll sigh, 'I could be wrong.' This sort of soul-searching can go on for ever, and frequently does!)

Librans' love of harmony and balance extends to matters of the heart, as you might expect. They must have luscious lovers (they must be physically fantastic), and the Libran man must have the most beautiful bird in town in tow, even if he's as ugly as a vulture himself (though he'll have a smashing smile and delicious dimples). Accuse Librans of this and they will say in a superior way that they're an intellectual Air sign, and so plump for personality, first and foremost. But you try to get a Libran to go out with someone who's no oil painting, but has bags of bounce and bonhomie, and see what happens. That's right. *Nothing!*

SCORPIO – 24 OCTOBER–22 NOVEMBER

Listen. Do you want to know a secret? (Where have I heard that line before?) Do you promise not to tell? Scorpios are ace! Their coolness can be captivating, and their furtiveness fascinating. And they're so laid-back it's luscious!

Scorpios have more undercurrents than a conger eel. You never know what makes them tick because they never give you a clue. (Is it clockwork or quartz?) They sit looking enigmatic, and you wonder what on earth they're thinking about!

In fact, enigmatic is the supreme Scorpio word. The normal give-away for this Plutonic sign is the eyes, which are like deep pools – you wonder what's going on below the surface. Scorpios are like icebergs; after all, if you combine their element, Water, with their Fixed quality, what do you get but ice?

Aries and Scorpio share the ancient rulership of mighty Mars, yet their temperaments are as different as chalk and cheese. Ariens have flashes of Fiery fury, and act on impulse (they'll suddenly strangle you with a sock). Scorpios, though, simmer and smoulder on the back burner of life's cooker, plotting and planning how to get even with you. And they'll manage it in the end! Scorpios have psychological power, and use it to the full whenever they can. (They could manipulate Machiavelli!)

Never underestimate a Scorpio. This is a phantasmagorically profound placing for a person, and Scorpios are imbued with intensity. This is, after all, the sign of sex and death.

Death, for a Scorpio, isn't always something physical; instead these folk can kill off certain sections of their lives they no longer like in the twinkling of an eye. They can transform and transfigure their lives more than any other sign, making fresh starts with barely a backward glance. However, since this is the sign of obsessions, some Scorpios are fascinated by physical death, and can gad about graveyards, looking at the headstones and absorbing the atmosphere. They'll be engrossed and enthralled by the ritual of death, and almost have death wishes, because they can't wait to know what it's like on the other side. Other Scorpios go to the opposite extreme, and are petrified of popping off!

Make no mistake, this is a sign of such compulsion, obsession and profundity that some people find Scorpios hard to handle. Just thinking about their intense inquisitions, interrogations and investigations makes some folk's hair stand on end! Scorpios can be like an oil rig, drilling deep into the heart of the matter. (I wonder how many of the men are called Derrick?) And if you want to know what makes a Scorpio tick, you've got to do the same to them. Then you'll start to see what's submerged beneath that superficially serene surface. (A Scorpio may come across as cool, calm and collected, but underneath that elegant exterior is a sizzling selection of scorching sensations simply seething away!)

Power is very important to these Plutonians, but it's always gained in a secretive way. Scorpios operate behind the scenes; they love to manipulate others, but hate to be caught in the glare of the spotlight themselves.

But don't just think there's only one sort of Scorpio, who's like the Spanish Inquisition. There are three sides to the sign, from the angelic to the awful. Top of the list is the devout Dove. This is the Scorpio who believes in peace and tranquillity, and strives for it at all costs. (Perhaps even becoming a nun or a monk in the process.) Next comes the exciting Eagle – the daredevil hero who takes risks and laughs in the face of danger. Whether James or Jane Bond, this Scorpio works behind the scenes as a spy or a secret agent. (You can always spot 'em because they shin up drainpipes in the dark, clutching cartons of chocs between their teeth!) So far so good, I hear you say. But lastly comes the sly Snake, that slithers through the undergrowth of life, then slinks out when you least expect it, and buries its fangs in your ankle. Ouch! These are the mass-murderers, the Charles Mansons of the world. (No wonder Scorpios can get a bad name!)

Luckily for the rest of us, that is the lowest level to which a Scorpio can sink. (It's the lowest level to which anyone can sink!) Higher-minded Scorpios choose to follow a positive path, seeking out the spiritual side of life. But a truly negative Scorpio will turn to black magic to fulfil that pulverising passion for power, taking a macabre interest in things most people shy away from. Once you've totally understood a complex Scorpio you'll have solved one of astrology's most ancient mysteries, and be shown sensational sights of life that no other sign can offer.

SAGITTARIUS – 23 NOVEMBER–21 DECEMBER

Talk about clumsy! If Sagittarians aren't putting both feet in it verbally, they're doing it physically, and landing up to their necks in trouble. If you ask an Archer round for afternoon tea, don't get out the best china. It'll only get broken. (Use some plastic plates instead.) Your Sagittarian pal will rush into the room and trip over the tea table, sending the cups and saucers flying in all directions. Then, to add insult to injury, as your mate dashes off for a dishcloth to mop up the mess, he or she will step on a cream cake and crunch it into the carpet. Still, having your residence wrecked is often better than hearing the truth about yourself, Sagittarian style. Your friend can say 'I saw someone who looked just like you yesterday.' However, before you feel pleased, and start to preen, wait for the punchline. 'Then I realised it was someone else, because you've got more spots.' See what I mean?

But let's look on the bright side – something that's second nature to our jovial pals. Sagittarians are incurable optimists (their beer bottles are always half full, never half empty), and they will inject others with their infectious enthusiasm, given half a chance. If you're feeling really down in the dumps, your Sagittarian pal will bounce up, tell you a joke or two and try to get you giggling again. Go on, give 'em a grin! Jupiter, the planet that rules these Archers, makes them magnificently merry, and they'll try to jolly everyone else along too. The terrific thing about them is that they usually succeed. You can't mooch about moping for long when there's an Archer around.

Because this is the polar sign of garrulous Gemini, Sagittarians are also blessed with the gift of the gab, and can talk the hind leg off a donkey. But there is a mighty difference between these two signs. Astrologically, Gemini is the lower-minded sign, dealing with subjects superficially and knowing a little about a lot, while Sagittarius is the opposite, full of philosophy and worldly wisdoms. (In ancient mythology, the Centaur – the Sagittarius symbol – was the master of teaching and healing.) During a deep discussion with an Archer, you'll find that they're searching for the meaning of life, and will ponder on the problem all through their existence. ('What's it all about, Alfie?' is definitely the Sagittarian song!) Faiths and beliefs are all-important to Archers.

Now, it's not for nothing that Sagittarius is the sign of the Archer. There's the hunter, poised with his bow and arrow, all a-quiver, taking aim at a target. Archers do this throughout their lives (always aiming for the bull's-eye), but the trouble is they often aim too high, and miss the target by miles. They set their sights too high (literally!). Sometimes, of course, an Archer will get it right first time, but usually life to these folk is like a rerun of the Battle of Hastings, with arrows flying in all directions. (If you're called Harold, you should head for the hills!)

It's all gigantic Jupiter's doing. Because he's the largest planet in the heavens, he gives some of these Sagittarians ideas above their stations. This can be a terrific trait, because it means that the Sagittarian is always striving for better things. But some Centaurs can go to the opposite extreme and exaggerate everything they come into contact with. As a result, they get everything out of proportion; they bounce about, blowing their own bugles, believing the world can't turn without them. You see, Jupiter knows no bounds – and neither do Sagittarians. (The world doesn't just end at Ambridge for these Archers!)

This is the universal sign, and all Archers are tantalised by travel and the thought of far-flung corners of the globe. Think of the Sagittarians you know. You'll find that lots of them went round the world as soon as they could, or lived in a foreign country at some point in their lives. (Their passports contain more stamps than a Stanley Gibbons catalogue!) This desire to get out and see the world for themselves can be the making of positive Sagittarians. Negative Archers, though, can wax lyrical about their exotic adventures, name-dropping like mad, so it sounds as though they spent a weekend at the White House, when actually they only whizzed past it on a bus.

Jupiter is the planet of luck and opportunity, and some Archers are just like cats, with nine lives. (Some of them are so accident-prone, they need all the help they can get!) You may think they're gauche and rude, but they call it being honest! They make the most of every opportunity that arises, and can often spot a chance when others don't think it's there. Sometimes that'll be their brilliant perception and vision, and other times it'll be blind faith and living in cloud-cuckoo-land. It's up to the Archer to decipher the mystical Morse code.

Meet a positive Sagittarian and you will be fulfilled in many ways, and imbued with a zest and a zeal for living. But a negative Archer can be crafty, or will let you down in some way or other, whether emotionally or materially. These folk can waste everyone's time, and will bite off more than they can chew. All Sagittarians need challenges; they need to know where to aim their celestial bows and arrows so they can hit the target fair and square. After all, it's much better to climb the ladder of life, rung by rung, than to take a flying leap at it and miss by miles!

CAPRICORN – 22 DECEMBER–20 JANUARY

Right, repeat after me, 'Capricorns are captivating.' Say it again. Got it? Good. Now remember it, and forget what you might have heard about these folk being morose and melancholic. You will find some Goats with a grouse, because there are positive and negative folks in every sign, but a together Goat can be gorgeous.

Let's get the worst over first with this sign. Some Capricorns can be the original wet blankets, moaning and misanthropic, complaining and carping, and generally being gloomy old things. You'll look at them and think 'I don't want to know you.' But if you bother to get to know them, you can have the time of your life. Talk about giggle!

One of the tremendous traits of this bunch is their superb sense of humour and wit that's as dry as a bone, but much more fun. They can take the mickey out of everything – including themselves, which makes them very endearing indeed. And they really do act the goat, making you laugh until your sides split. Once you've glimpsed the sensational side of this sign, you can turn a blind eye to its more *triste* traits, because you'll have found the silver lining to the Capricorn cloud. (And the crock of gold at the end of the rainbow, if the Goat has Taurus rising.)

Some negative Capricorns can pick holes in everything – even if they hit the jackpot at bingo, they'll moan about having to spend all that money. The poor things can't express their emotions, either, and will bottle up all their feelings and frustrations.

When you meet a Capricorn, expect them to act older than their years. Goats age in the opposite way to the rest of us, behaving as if they were fifty when they're only five, and seven when they're seventy. This means that Capricorns make elderly-seeming babies and young-at-heart pensioners. When the rest of us are being put out to grass, Goats are just coming into their own!

This is a sign that believes in experience, with a capital 'E'. They never have an easy life until they've blown out all the candles on their thirtieth birthday cakes. Until then, life will have been one long struggle; the only way for them to survive is to learn by experience. (Capricorns hate wasting *anything*!) Many of them will have had cramped childhoods, awful adolescences and terrible twenties. But they'll have terrific thirties, fantastic forties – even naughty nineties!

There are two types of Goat – the ones who cavort and curvet up the crags to the summit of their own mountainsides, and the ones who are domestic, and like to potter about their own pieces of pasture, never straying far from the fireside. Capricorns are Cardinal, making them astoundingly ambitious, and even the domestic ones will be determined to do well. Success for them, though, isn't totally based on boodle (although they'd never refuse owt for nowt!); honour, public position and status all smell sweet to them.

Capricorns need security, which they get from the tried, true and tested. They love history, and anything with a past (this could mean you), because then they feel safe. Capricorns are conservative, canny and cautious, and are suspicious of new-fangled things, until they get used to them. They hate to fly in the face of convention.

They're very wary of wearing out their wallets, too. They believe that if they take care of the farthings, the pennies will look after themselves. More positive Goats would call themselves careful, and will be generous with their loot when they've got it, and laugh about it when they haven't. (Always with a note of caution in their grin!)

Guilt is a very Goaty thing, and some Capricorns thrive on it, putting everyone through the mill, including themselves. They can set themselves impossibly high ideals, and almost galactic goals, and then hate themselves when they fail to reach them. Because just as they hate waste, they also can't abide failure. (It's a good job they're imbued with endurance and endeavour!) They are deeply determined and disciplined, so can drive themselves to hit heights others only dream of.

But not all Goats are quite so positive. Some delight in the doldrums, like grumpy old Eeyore in *Winnie the Pooh* – a donkey who's always down in the dumps. But still everyone adored him. In fact, with a little understanding, you are sure to have fun with even the most morose Goats: laugh with them, but never at them, and you'll never feel down!

AQUARIUS – 21 JANUARY–19 FEBRUARY

You learn a whole new vocabulary when you meet an Aquarian. Forget about the usual words, and ponder on ones like 'contrary', 'bizarre', 'radical' and 'outrageous'. In fact, you'd do well to remember them, because you're going to need them.

Before I go any further, let's get one thing straight. Well, two if you're going to be pedantic. (And if you are, make sure it's not in front of an Aquarian. They aren't particularly pleased by pedantic people.) There are two types of Aquarians: those ruled by Saturn and those ruled by Uranus. It's strange, I know, but then a lot of people think Aquarians are strange . . . (Watch it, because I'm one of them.)

Saturn is the ancient ruler of Aquarius; when rebellious, revolutionary Uranus was revealed he was given to the Sun sign most fitting that description – Airy Aquarius. (Some people think Aquarius is a Water sign, but it isn't. Its symbol may be the Water Carrier, but it is actually the third of the Air signs. Confusing, isn't it?)

Saturn Aquarians tend to be conservative, reliable and positive pillars of proper society. You won't catch them wearing lampshades for hats, unless you've spiked their sherry. If that sounds a bit like Capricorn, you're right. Saturn Aquarians do have a lot of Capricorn's characteristics, so if you think you know one, turn back to the previous chapter and have a gander at the Goats.

I'm going to deal mostly with Uranus-ruled Aquarians here. (Usually, you will discover which planet is strongest by studying the birth chart. Sometimes it will be easier – you may meet an Aquarian who is so Saturnine it's not true, or so unusual that they have to be Uranian. Unless they're just plain mad.)

An ancient astrological adage says you can't tell Aquarians anything because they know it already, and very often will tell you so. One of the negative qualities of Aquarians is their one-upmanship. You can meet an Aquarian mate for a meal, and arrive in a wheelchair with your bonce in a big bandage. As the waiter whizzes you to the table, you will smile through your layers of lint, expecting a sudden show of sympathy. The Aquarian will look up, and ask you what happened. So far so good. After you've mumbled in a muffled manner that you were weeding your window box and fell off, fracturing your femur and splitting your skull, the Aquarian will sigh, say 'Oh, is that all?' and go on to recount how they once broke both arms *and* both legs, wrecked their ribs and biffed their back, while morris dancing at Kew Gardens. It can make you mad, but don't kick them with your cast, because it'll hurt you more than them. The negative Saturn Aquarian can be like the negative Capricorn, and be plagued with pessimism, downcast by depression and doubt, and worn out with worry.

The two halves of Aquarius are so very different. If the Saturn type is black and white, then the Uranian Aquarian is all the colours in the spectrum. They can be completely confusing, contrary, unpredictable and incomprehensible – qualities that set them completely apart from their Saturn brothers and sisters. Uranus Aquarians are all of a jitter, rushing here and there, and constantly changing their moods. They remind me of Merlin, popping up when you least expect it. In astrology, Uranus is known as the great awakener, as if a magic wand had been waved, the word 'abracadabra' said. He will create change in something that was static. So, the Uranus-ruled Aquarian is ceaselessly craving change.

On a positive level, this means that the Aquarian is eternally excited and exhilarated by what may lie round the corner, and there may be sudden changes of career, luck or partners when Uranus decides to stage a shake-up. Negatively, an Aquarian will want to change things just for the sake of it, because he or she longs to rock the boat. Routine can be anathema to an Aquarian; the Saturn Aquarian, on the other hand, may find it rather reassuring. This is the quintessence of the Aquarian quandary – complete contradiction, with one half of the sign panting for pastures new, and the other following the furrow.

You never know what's going to happen next with an Aquarian. Life can be a lot of fun, or you can find it very tiring. Aquarians are unconventional, but they are also original, and along with Geminis, are said to be the geniuses of the zodiac. They can be inventive and brilliantly clever, although sometimes they are spectacular in such a strange way, so abstract and off at such a tremendous tangent, that no one knows what they're talking about! Aquarians are really born way ahead of their time. (After all, they laughed at Christopher

Columbus when he said the world was round!) Other people, who are rather less free-thinking and original, will conclude that they are completely cranky.

Another Aquarian contradiction is that although Water Carriers are said to be humanitarians, they can be emotional ice cubes in the cocktail of life, and don't easily express their emotions. They *can* be humanitarian – helping others, sending cash to charities, or being affectionate on a large scale – yet find their own close relationships difficult to cope with. Aquarius is a Fixed sign, so it can be intolerably inflexible and intransigent. For all their brainpower and brilliance, Aquarians can be staggeringly stupid and stubborn, standing their ground over a long-lost cause and unable to admit they are in the wrong.

Since Aquarius is an Air sign, the Aquarian will be much more mesmerised by a marriage of the minds than a partnership of passion and physical fulfilment. Very often, they pick the most unlikely-looking person for a partner, because they will have chosen them for their mind rather than for anything else. Aquarians can have some very avant-garde relationships! (Ever heard of Beauty and the beast? And guess who's playing Beauty!)

Aquarians think of the future a great deal; often when they have just crossed one hurdle, they will think 'Where will this lead?' and 'I wonder what's going to happen next?' And this brings me to another Aquarian attribute. They are the only sign to answer a question with a question. Ask an Aquarian if it's raining, and he or she will ask you why you want to know. (A Piscean would say yes, and offer to lend you their green gamp.) The first word Aquarian children learn is 'Why?', and they will continue to ask that question all through their lives.

You can never get really close to an Aquarian. Unless they have plenty of Pisces and Taurus in their charts to warm them up, they can be aloof and cold and difficult to cuddle. But for all that, life with an Aquarian, either as a pal or a partner, will never be dull, and that's something to think about!

PISCES – 20 FEBRUARY–20 MARCH

Saintly Pisces! Some of these Fish should be canonised, they are so far advanced along the road to spiritual enlightenment. (Others still seem to be waiting at the heavenly bus stop!)

Now, there are two sorts of Pisceans; this last sign of the zodiac is ruled by two planets – jocular, jaunty Jupiter, and nebulous, nectarine Neptune. The Jupiter-ruled Pisceans are very akin to Sagittarians, because they share the same ruler. But Jupiterian Pisceans aren't prone to the flights of fancy shown by Sagittarians. Their ruler represents wealth and good fortune, and the Jupiterian Fish will always have an eye on these things. In fact, Pisces brings out these Jupiterian qualities beautifully, making the Fish full of fun and clever at bringing in the boodle. Negatively, there will be a tendency towards overexpansion, whether in girth, mirth, or wheeling and dealing. But these Jupiterian Fish do burst with bounteous bonhomie, and can be gloriously generous and marvellously magnanimous.

Because of the saintly side of this sign, Pisceans can be very devout and pious. (It depends on the Fish whether that will make you awed or bored.) If they are ruled by Jupiter, they will accept the faith or religion they have been brought up in. A Neptunian Piscean, however, will be more unusual, even mystical, and may find Eastern religions especially attractive.

This is a profoundly psychic sign, and the Piscean should use this ability positively to live a better life. Many Fish become fascinated by black magic and the occult, like Scorpios, because they are seduced by secrecy. But, generally, Pisceans have an inspiration that can draw them wholeheartedly into the realms of the positive supernatural and mystical. They are also intensely interested in spiritualism, because it helps them to get in touch with that unseen lot they feel so much a part of.

Neptunian Pisceans waft along on clouds, daydreaming away to their heart's content. They really aren't part of this world at all! (This isn't the same as Aquarians, who are futuristic, and one step ahead of everyone else. Pisceans are unworldly in a filigree, fantasial way.) These Fish will appear magical and mystical, and they can be profoundly artistic and unworldly sometimes, to the point of being gullible or geniuses. Lord Byron had powerful Piscean placings, and Mozart and Chopin both had the Sun in this sign, as does Rudolph Nureyev, who brought a whole new concept to ballet. (And to tights. Pisceans love to leave something to the imagination!)

What you must remember about Neptune is that this planet gives an illusory image to everything it encounters. Neptune represents something that can never be captured or held on to. Think of an intangible will-o'-the-wisp, or a piece of thistledown floating through the air that always eludes you, and you have the perfect picture of Pisceans.

They can bring this quality into their everyday lives, imbuing them with illusion, and smothering them in strange sea mists. You will think you're looking at one thing, then the shadows shift and you discover you're seeing something quite different.

Everything that Neptune does is intensified in an ethereal way, so Neptunian Pisceans will be hypersensitive, and as fragile as a butterfly's wing. They can feel neurotically nauseated by anything ugly, whether it's society, sights, sounds or situations. Some Fishy folk can't stand the slightest facial flaw, let alone anything else. (Better talk to them with your head hidden!) Yet such is their spiritual self-awareness, that often they will devote their lives to the very vocations which you'd think they couldn't bear. For example, they might join the prison service (but not behind bars!), look after the old and infirm, and the mentally and physically handicapped. These positive Pisceans force themselves to face up to their phobias, and bring some good out of them. (Other Pisceans will only want the erotic, exotic, seductive and sumptuous side of life, and none of the unpleasant parts.)

I can hear you saying 'That sounds like Libra!', and you'd be right. Neptune is said to be the higher octave of Venus, a sort of top C of the zodiac. It's like a dog whistle, which has a note that's too high for humans to hear. And this is what Neptunian natives are like – they're listening to a high-pitched tone that the rest of us can't catch. Equally, Jupiter is said to be the higher octave of Mercury, and Jupiterian folk can understand all the deeper things of life that a Mercury-ruled person skims over. Between them, Mercury and Jupiter rule the four Mutable signs – Gemini, Virgo, Sagittarius and Pisces. (Interesting, isn't it?).

Neptune is a fantastically fantasial figure. On a positive level, its influence means that Neptunians can be wonderful writers, divine dancers and profound poets. (And incurable romantics.) But negatively, they can be monstrously Machiavellian, playing one person off against another. Some of them make Lucretia Borgia look like Little Bo Peep; they can be malicious and malevolent, vicious and venomous, treacherous and two-faced. (They have a wonderful way of believing their own fibs and fables.) And this is how we get the symbol of Pisces, which is a fish swimming in different directions. Pisceans are either way up at the top of the tree or at rock bottom; either the nurse helping the drug addict or the addict himself.

Fish are vulnerable, and can be victims of the unknown, murky depths of their imaginations and subconscious minds. They are either inspired, or they're the dregs of the earth, who rely on society to look after them.

There's no getting away from it. This sign is a mystery, but not in a Scorpionic way. Rather, it's unworldly, in a delicious, delectable, gossamer-like way. There is a floaty, flimsy veil hiding what is really going on in the Piscean life. The Fish can inhabit a very weird world, and the worst thing Pisceans can do is to drift along on an aimless sea, when their phobias, fetishes and fixations may well get the better of them. They are very impressionable indeed, and negative Pisceans will be plagued by psychosomatic problems that they have brought on themselves. Positive Pisceans can direct that abundant artistry, that magnificent mysticism, into a brilliant conclusion. Or they can live such serene spiritual lives that nothing else matters, because their tremendous inner peace brings them total fulfilment.

Think of your Fishy friends, and you'll realise that something strange sets them apart from everyone else. You can't put your finger on it, but you know it's there. Remember those sea mists. One minute the view is as clear as a bell, the next you're sinking into a ferocious fog! It's a magical, mystical mystery.

RUSSELL'S RELATIONSHIP GUIDE

LEO MAN AND ARIES WOMAN

What a terrific twosome! It's a pairing made in paradise when you two start seeing each other, as you both share the same ideas about fun, frolics and having a jolly good time. The only trouble is that your bank manager could put a damper on things when you start running up debts and overdrafts and landing yourself in hot water financially. With the combination of your love of luxury and your Arien amourette's impulsive streak, your boodle bags don't stand a chance! Even so, you're a terrifically creative couple, so if the coffers run low why not put your heads together and dream up a few money-making schemes? Because you're both Fire signs, sexual sparks fly when you two get together, but unless you can understand that it's OK to be attracted to other folk as well as each other, you'll exchange a few harsh words too!

LEO MAN AND TAURUS WOMAN

Loyalty? It goes without saying when you two start stepping out together, as you're both fundamentally faithful and true. The problems start when that fidelity spills over into other areas of your affair, making you both determined, dogmatic and even dictatorial. Your Taurean gal doesn't welcome any sort of change in her world, and you believe that you're right – always! It can be hopeless if you try to have a discussion or debate, because it usually ends in stalemate, with both of you too proud or pedantic to back down one inch. Once you can learn to compromise, you'll be well on the way to a wonderful relationship in which you can pamper and pander to each other's needs and desires. You'll adore the weay she always looks a treat, and she'll look after you as only a Bullette can. Smashing!

LEO MAN AND GEMINI WOMAN
Love and laughter – that's what you can look forward to when a Gemini girl takes your fancy, and even if you're just platonic pals you'll have a ball whenever you get together. You share the same sense of humour, so you can usually find something to laugh at – as long as you're not the butt of the joke! Your Gemini girl will revel in your warmth and big-hearted bonhomie and you'll enjoy the way her mind hops from subject to subject and keeps you entertained (how does she know so many fascinating facts?). All the same, you believe in fidelity, faithfulness and loyalty, and won't take kindly to your Mercurial maiden chatting up every Tom, Dick and Harry whenever she gets the chance. It may only be for fun, but you might not see it like that! Never mind, because it won't take much to get you both laughing again, and that's your recipe for romantic success.

LEO MAN AND CANCER WOMAN
''S wonderful, 's marvellous' – that's the song you'll sing when you and a Crabette are a Cupidic couple, and who can blame you? It's a paradisaical partnership, because you've got stacks in common to draw you together. For a start, your Cancerian needs to know that her amour is faithful, so she'll be quids in with loyal and loving you. You two will stick by each other come what may, and if you plight your troth you will want to be together forever. The prospect of hearing the patter of tiny feet will thrill you both to the core, and you'll dote on your wee bairns, bringing them up in an adoring atmosphere of love and laughter. They're almost bound to have an old-fashioned childhood, with your Cancerian lass staying in the nest with the wee ones while you go out to earn the daily bread. Talk about happy families!

LEO MAN AND LEO WOMAN
Forget the three Rs when you're one half of this Cupidic couple and start concentrating on the three Ls instead – love, laughter and

luxury. These are the prime ingredients for amour Leo-style – not that you need to be told that! Once you two passionate and pleasure-loving pussycats meet you'll be delighted to discover that you both belong to the same Sun sign because it'll mean that you both want the same things out of life (unless one of you is a strange and shady sort). And what is it that you want? Why, the very best that money can buy, of course! You also long for amour, affection, appreciation and applause – things that each of you should be able to give the other. Although you're fundamentally faithful, there's nothing you like better than a wee flirt or fandango with a femme fatale, and you may purr with pride when your pretty paramour turns *hommes*' heads in her direction, but you'll soon start to snarl when she gives as good as she gets. Remember that your Leonine love is a very liberated lady, and then you'll be all set for a purr-fect pairing.

LEO MAN AND VIRGO WOMAN

Talk about the odd couple! You may be next-door neighbours on the astrological wheel of life, but that could be where the resemblance ends when you join forces with a Virgo lady. Let's face it, as a Leo lad you're extravagant, ebullient, expansive and expensive, while your Mercurial maiden is much more modest, meek and mild. Once you progress from billing and cooing to cuddling and canoodling you could hit a severe snag when you discover your discreet damsel finds you too hot to handle, and you could have to tone down the ardent aura that surrounds all your sexual shenanigans. Even so, you'll adore your pretty and pert little lass and the way she's so decorative and delectable, though her painstaking and pedantic ways could send you into a frenzy of frustration.

LEO MAN AND LIBRA WOMAN

Smashing! It's a terrific twosome when you two lovebirds start singing a song of amour together, and it'll seem as though you were meant to meet. After all, you do both belong to the two signs of love, so it's bound to be sugar and spice and all things nice when your hearts entwine in an amorous embrace. Your Fiery emotions will be fanned by the Airy ardour of your Venusian valentine till you're both in a fervour of potent passion that carries you away on a cloud of bliss. There's only one problem, and that's the way you're both practised in the art of pretending that everything's hunky-dory even when it isn't. You're both idealists and hate to admit that anything's wrong, but you've got to mix some realism into your romantic recipe if you want this coupling to be a captivating and charming Cupidic concoction. Bon appetit!

LEO MAN AND SCORPIO WOMAN
Sizzle, sizzle! Sexually you're the tops together and it can take all your willpower to make you two bourée out of bed once you've slipped between the sheets (or anywhere else for that matter!). Whenever the kissing stops, even temporarily, it's that willpower that can start causing trouble galore between you. You see, because you're both Fixed folk, you're very strong-minded, so once you've reached a decision nothing and no one can budge you one inch. That can be difficult enough when it's just one of you who's so immovable and intransigent, but it's disaster when you're both digging in your heels and being resolute. If you want things to last, you've both got to climb down from your high horses and learn a little give-and-take. What's more, you've got to respect your Scorpio sweetheart's viewpoint as well as your own.

LEO MAN AND SAGITTARIUS WOMAN
Got your passports handy? When you two pair up together it'll be enjoyment all the way, and what you'll love most of all is jetting off to faraway places with strange-sounding names, especially if they're full of Eastern promise or so select that no one's ever heard of 'em. (Let's face it, you both love stealing a march on your pals!) Well, you're both Fire signs, so you're full of exuberance, enthusiasm and enterprise and try to enjoy life as much as possible. Things won't get too expensive if you've never had much money to play with, but if you suddenly switch from having a lot of loot to a little you'll carry on as though nothing's happened and you've got all the cash in the world. Emotionally you're marvellously matched and sexually you're a perfect pair. Who could ask for anything more?

LEO MAN AND CAPRICORN WOMAN
'Hey, good looking!' That's what you'll say when you first clap eyes on a sleek, soignée and sophisticated Capricorn lass (unless she's one of the few Girl goats who look as though they've climbed through a hedge backwards, in which case you may not even give her the time of day). As a proud Leo lad you love having a decora-

tive damsel on your arm, and you couldn't have picked a better bet than this Saturnalian siren. The problems will start (yes, I know there always seems to be a snag!) when you switch from being social to sexual, as your lady love may be very reserved when it comes to romance. Be patient if she finds it hard to let her hair down, as she's worried about committing herself to someone and then being rejected. It could take a lot of hard work to win her trust and her heart, but once you've got them you can begin building a relationship that'll last for ever and a day.

LEO MAN AND AQUARIUS WOMAN

Ain't life grand? That what you'll be saying when you fall for an Aquarian dame, and who can blame you? She knows exactly how to keep you on your toes, always getting you guessing about what she's going to get up to next. One minute she'll be off to save the whale and the next she'll be reclining in the lap of luxury, and as long as her love for you doesn't falter for a second (you're far too faithful and fervent to stand for that) you'll happily follow her fads and foibles till the cows come home – or, in your case, the Lions! Even so, unless you can take it in your stride when she blows hot and cold in the boudoir, you could hit some snags and setbacks if you're not careful. If she says she's having a celibate week, the last thing you should do is sulk or stomp off and slam the bedroom door behind you. Instead, be understanding and wait for the seven days to pass. Who knows, next time she could be feeling very hot-blooded indeed!

LEO MAN AND PISCES WOMAN

Love unlimited! That's what you can expect when you fall for a fabulous female Fish, and your relationship will be as rhapsodic and romantic as the Hollywood musical in its heyday. You'll be lulled along by a lullaby of love that'll make you want to spend all your spare time snuggled up in a warm wonderland of your very own. Who cares about the rest of the world when you two can be together? In fact, once you amour gets off the ground your Piscean paramour could come on a wee bit too strong even for lusty old you, and the depth and strength of her emotions could leave you speechless sometimes. In return, she'll love your wooing ways and the little games you play together. Since you're two of the most artistic signs in the celestial set-up, developing your creativity together can forge a lasting link between you.

LEO WOMAN AND ARIES MAN

Ring-a-ding-ding! The bells are ringing when you get together with an ardent Arien amour, but there's one thing that could put the clappers on the coupling. Can you afford it? Neither of you is exactly restrained when it comes to spending your loot, so when the two of you get together the pounds and pence will fly in all directions! With your luxury-loving ways and your Martian man's daredevil approach to life, you could run through more money in a month than you earn in a year! He'll adore it when you look decorative and dazzling, and you'll be thrilled at the way he naturally takes the lead. What's more, because you're both Fire signs, you're driven by red-hot emotions. Sexually, things couldn't be better! When the sign of love (that's you!) meets the sign of sex (that's him!), it's passion personified.

LEO WOMAN AND TAURUS MAN

We shall not be moved – that's your theme song when you pair up with a boy Bull. Because you're both Fixed signs of the zodiac, you both believe in standing your ground and sticking to your guns whenever there's a disagreement or discussion. Neither of you likes giving in or admitting you might be wrong, which can lead to lots of stormy scenes and tempestuous tirades! There can also be some pretty sultry scenarios whenever you sidle off to the bedroom, and your gift for amour combines with your terrific Taurean's potent passion. What a captivating combination! However, you could hit big trouble with this Venusian valentine if he believes a woman's place is in the home, while you prefer to be out on the town or having smashing spending sprees with his loot. Better come to a compromise or, better still, persuade him to join in the fun!

LEO WOMAN AND GEMINI MAN

Snap, crackle and pop! Whichever joint you're in, it's bound to be jumping if you two are there, because a captivating chemistry takes place whenever a Gemini and a Leo get together. Whether you're perfect pals or each other's heart's desire, there's a ravishing rapport between you. There's no doubt it's style all the way when you meet a Gemini man, but watch out for that bank balance or you'll both start spending money as though it's going out of fashion. You'll love it if he's got a costly car, luxurious lifestyle or the very latest in designer gadgets, gifts and good things. What's more, he'll win your respect in two seconds flat if he can walk into a pub, club or restaurant and know more of the folk there than you do! In return, you'll be able to teach your Gemini swain a few Leonine lessons about love and affection and help him develop his innate emotions, though you won't like it if he starts practising with anyone but you! If he's faithful, you could be together forever.

LEO WOMAN AND CANCER MAN

Magnificent! It's love that brings you two together, as you're both driven by the need for affection and amour, and if you play your cards right you'll still be a devoted duo in your dotage! You both love the way you can give vent to the full flood of your feelings without having to hold back – what a romantic couple you are! Sexually you're inspired, and it's a very tactile, loving and giving combination when you slip between the sheets. All the same, your Cancerian chap has got to treat you in the right way, or he'll soon hear all about it! You won't take kindly to him hoarding or hiding all the housekeeping whenever you fancy a spending spree. Instead, he's got to smile, not squirm, when you buy up everything in sight, even though you can go overboard sometimes. Things will soon go downhill if he's a bit of a Scrooge or stick-in-the-mud, as you'll trot off into the sunset with one toss of your marvellous mane, leaving him all on his ownsome!

LEO WOMAN AND LEO MAN

When you get together it's like a Hollywood spectacular, but with both of you playing the romantic lead! After all, because you both belong to the regal sign of Leo, neither of you likes playing second fiddle, and even if you live in a two-up two-down dwelling in Dundee, you'll both behave as though it's Holyroodhouse. What a majestic mating this is! As a huge-hearted Leo lass you'll love the way your kingly sweetheart is strong on the surface and as cuddly as a kitten underneath. When you go out on the town (which will be as often as possible) you'll want to be seen at all the best shindigs and soirées, even if they do cost a mint. There's only one fly in this expensive ointment – who's going to wear the trousers? You'll both want to call the shots, so take it in turns to be king or queen of your castle, and you'll be as happy as sand boys and girls for ever more.

LEO WOMAN AND VIRGO MAN

Money may make the world go round, but it can call a halt to this amorous alliance almost before it's begun. You see, as a Leo lady you love the best things in life, and they can come very expensive indeed. Now, your Virgoan valentine is many things, but a big spender ain't one of 'em. The sight of you choosing the swankiest seats for a star-studded show (surely he doesn't expect you to sit in the stalls when you could be in a box?) or giving the bargain baked beans the slip in the supermarket and heading straight for the salmon steaks instead (*how* much?), is enough to bring on one of his funny turns. If you two want to live happily ever after you've got to come to a compromise about everything from shopping to sex. You can be a bit too blatant in the bedroom for this modest male, especially if he likes leaving the light off. On the other hand he could be the sort of Virgo who has a few sexual tricks up his sleeve (or somewhere similar) that'll keep you happy and contented.

LEO WOMAN AND LIBRA MAN

What a combination! It's like Nelson Eddy and Jeanette Mac-Donald all over again when you two meet, and it won't be long before you're united in an amorous aura of adoration. After all, how could you resist each other when you belong to the two astrological signs of love? What's more, your adoration of beautiful things could bring you together (well, you've chosen each other, which must prove something!), and your abode will be full of silks, satins and the finest frills and furbelows that money (or credit cards) can buy. You'll start drinking champagne instead of shandy long before you can afford it but you'll say you're getting into practice for when that day comes. The only trouble is that you'll probably use the bills that plop through your letter box to light the candles for yet another romantic dinner *à deux*! It's hard for you two to come down to earth and who can blame you?

LEO WOMAN AND SCORPIO MAN

Passion and power – those are the main ingredients in your romantic recipe but will it result in a mixture that curdles your stomach or warms the cockles of your heart? As far as sex is concerned, you'll be stupefied and spellbound by the fantastic fireworks and frissons that are sparked off whenever you two get together, but you may not be quite so keen on the battles for power that can take place when you disagree over something. After all, you do adore having the upper hand in a relationship, while your Scorpio swain needs to be the power behind the scenes, and that can cause fireworks of a very different sort indeed. While you're trying to get your own way by pulling out all the dramatic stops and staging an Oscar-winning performance of being horrendously hurt, your other half will have turned his passion into permafrost in the hope that he'll freeze you out. Better learn the art of compromise before your pairing reaches the bitter end.

LEO WOMAN AND SAGITTARIUS MAN

It'll be roses all the way when an amorous Archer sweeps you off your feet, though you'd better not believe everything he tells you till you see it with your own eyes. (He can be a past master at exaggeration.) Even if his Mercedes does turn out to be a Mini, you'll enjoy the way you whiz up and down motorways on the lookout for exciting new places to visit. What a good job you've both got a taste of adventure, though you'll be happiest when there's a dash of delicious luxury to accompany the thrills and spills, and you could draw the line when your try-anything-once amour suggests camping under the stars with nowt but your love to keep you warm. After all, your idea of roughing it can be travelling by train instead of taxi! Never mind, because you'll still have a smashing time together, whether you're in a field or a five-star hotel.

LEO WOMAN AND CAPRICORN MAN

Businesswise it's brill when you two join forces, but romantically it could be another story, and not necessarily one that ends happily ever after! You see, your feelings are at opposite ends of the emotional spectrum, and while you're demonstrative and believe in displaying your affections, your Capricorn chap prefers to keep a stiff upper lip and not betray a flicker of feeling. Woe betide you if you fling your arms around him in public or give him a smacking kiss in front of his kith and kin, and after a while you could feel very fed up with having to restrain your romancing. What's more, he could soon see sex as just one of the many duties he has to perform, and a hot-blooded Lioness like you won't take kindly to that at all! You also won't appreciate the way he seems to be wedded to his work as well as you, and though you'll enjoy the fruits of his labours, you won't want to be a grass widow for long. Better do some straight talking before you decide there are plenty more fish in the sea. Oh, alright then, Goats in the paddock!

LEO WOMAN AND AQUARIUS MAN

Ten out of ten! That's how you rate on the compatibility scale, which is hardly surprising 'cos you're astrological opposites, which means that you get on like a house on fire. Once you switch from friends to lovers, though, you might have to change your mind about your Aquarian *homme* when you discover that he's not nearly as openly affectionate, ardent and amorous as you'd like. You adore being bowled over by demonstrations of passion and undying love, but you could wait a long time before your Aquarian amour behaves like a latter-day Rudolph Valentino. Instead, he'll have some very erratic emotions that will be lecherous one moment and laid back the next. If you want your liaison to last, you'll have to learn to live with his brand of Aquarian amour, and he'll have to show his lust and love more openly. Persevere with this pairing and you'll be delighted with the ravishing results!

LEO WOMAN AND PISCES MAN

This pairing could be perfect or pathetic, and it will all depend on the inner strength and will of your Fishy fella. As a Leo lady you like to call the shots in a relationship, but if your Piscean paramour is so weak and wishy-washy that you can twist him round your little finger you'll soon lose interest and move on to someone who's got a bit more backbone. Well, even you don't like it when things are too easy! If you've fallen for a Fish who knows his own mind and can stand up for himself, though, you'll both be in clover, as long as you don't try to rule the roost with a rod of iron. When it comes to sex, you'll be delighted with the soft and sensitive ways of your romantic Romeo, and glad that you've found a man who isn't frightened of showing his innermost and most intimate emotions.

VENUS AND YOU

The planet of love, beauty, harmony and all things artistic, Venus is a very important influence on our lives indeed. She's considered to be a particularly feminine planet, and is associated with the emotions, money, social life, possessions, partnerships, clothes and fashion.

Folk who have a strong Venus in their solar charts (for example, the Ascendant, Sun or Moon in Taurus or Libra) may be anything from stunningly attractive to very beautiful indeed, and they also have refined tastes, are gentle, placid, diplomatic, understanding and creative. On the other hand, people with negative Venusian traits can be lazy, overindulgent, soppy, too sweet for words or impractical. Luscious Venus also rules the throat, lower back and kidneys, and folk with strong Venusian placings are often blessed with beautiful voices and a deep love for or appreciation of music.

Although Venus rules the signs of Taurus and Libra, nevertheless she also has an important part to play in everyone's natal horoscope, for her placing and aspects will tell an astrologer volumes about a person's love life, artistic attributes, how strong their powers of attraction are and how they relate to others. If you've often wondered why you react amorously in a way that's contrary or contradictory to your Sun sign, it could well be because your natal Venus occupies a different sign, whether it's adjacent to or two signs

41

away from your own Sun sign. (Its close orbit to the Sun means it can never be further away than that.)

Well, whether you know the position of Venus in your own natal chart or not, following her progress through the starry skies in the coming year will still give you a helping hand where all loving liaisons and artistic affairs are concerned.

VENUS'S ENTRY INTO THE SIGNS IN 1993

from 1 January	Aquarius
4 January	enters Pisces
2 February	enters Aries
11 March	turns retrograde in Aries
22 April	turns direct in Aries
6 June	enters Taurus
6 July	enters Gemini
2 August	enters Cancer
27 August	enters Leo
21 September	enters Virgo
16 October	enters Libra
9 November	enters Scorpio
3 December	enters Sagittarius
26 December	enters Capricorn

VENUS'S PROGRESS THROUGH THE ZODIAC

It's easy to plot the progress of sweet Venus through the zodiac with the help of my chart. The zodiac consists of twelve houses, each ruled by a particular Sun sign. When velvety Venus occupies your Sun sign, she's said to be in your first solar house, and when she moves on to the next sign she occupies your second solar house, and so on until she's travelled right round the zodiac and returned to your Sun sign again.

Each time she changes houses and signs, Venus influences a different part of your life. For example, whenever she visits your Sun sign (your first solar abode), she makes you even more delectable, dazzling, debonair and delightful than usual. When she glides through a sign that's compatible with yours (and that means your third, fifth, ninth and eleventh houses), you feel happy and harmonious, and full of the joys of spring. However, when she traverses signs that aren't amenable to yours (in other words, your fourth, seventh and tenth houses), your loving feelings can take a slightly tricky turn, or you may even be too indulgent for your own good.

Using the picture of the zodiac wheel below, write in the number 1 by your Sun sign and continue in an anti-clockwise direction around the signs until you've completed them all. Then it will be easy for you to trace the primrose path of voluptuous Venus in 1993! Enjoy yourself!

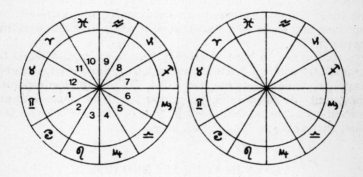

Astrological houses numbered for someone born with the Sun in Gemini.

Fill in this diagram and you'll be able to plot the course of Venus through each of your astrological houses. Simply write the number 1 by your Sun sign and continue in an anti-clockwise direction around the zodiac wheel until you have completed all twelve.

VENUS IN YOUR FIRST HOUSE

If you've got it, flaunt it! (And if you haven't, now's your chance to pretend you have!) Those are the mottoes to remember at the moment, for it's a terrific time to cash in on your innate charm and captivating charisma, and entrance everyone around you. Even if you'll never win a beauty contest, there's no excuse for not making a sterling effort to bring out your best assets and attributes.

Want to win someone round to your side, turn the head (and heart) of a prospective partner or just knock everyone dead with your wonderful ways? Then pull out all the stops and you'll be amazed at what you can do! If you're fed up with your current image, why not treat yourself to a flattering hairdo, a few trendy new togs or some modern make-up? Even the smallest change could make a big difference now, and boost your confidence no end at the same time!

All your dealings with others should benefit now from your easy-going and unaggressive attitude, making you a popular person to have around. Rather than stand up for your rights, you'll prefer to discuss things in a calm and collected way that's bound to see you coming up trumps. Acting as a go-between for others will also see you shine and make folk marvel at your reasonable and unruffled approach.

Getting down to hard work may be almost impossible at the moment, for you're much more interested in enjoying yourself than in applying your nose to the grindstone. Try to postpone important tasks until you're more in the mood for them, then surround yourself with friends, take a wee holiday or just have a lovely time being busy doing nothing. You'll have a ball!

VENUS IN YOUR SECOND HOUSE

A thing of beauty is a joy forever! That's how you feel at the moment, as you long to be surrounded by pretty possessions, arty antiques and those little luxuries that bring you happiness and harmony. If you don't already own them, you'll be scooting off to the shops before you can say 'I'll take it'! Quality, not quantity, is what you're after now, so you're likely to head for Harrods and cop out of the Co-op. You couldn't give a fig for a bargain now, for you firmly believe you get what you pay for. You could also go for the most gorgeous grub and grog you can find, or book a table at the best restaurant in town.

Sounds good, doesn't it? But there are some possible pitfalls to steer clear of along the way. To begin with, it'll be only too easy to spend what you haven't got now, for even if you start your shopping spree with good intentions you could soon come to grief. Let's face it, your willpower's fading fast at the moment and it'll peter out altogether at the first sight of a tempting treat or two! It's a grand chance to splash out a little loot, but don't fall victim to real extravagance if you haven't got the boodle to back it up! Unless your taste is always top notch, you'll need to be careful in another way too. You *could* show a superb artistic appreciation but on the other hand, once Venus has moved on, you may realise you've gone for things that are gaudy and garish. Whoops!

To look on the bright side, any negotiations with a financial flavour should go like clockwork, especially if you're clinching a deal or asking for a loan.

VENUS IN YOUR THIRD HOUSE

Personality plus! That's you at the moment, making you a grand person to have around and putting you high on everyone's list of favourite folk. It's your congenial, convivial and captivating ways that are attracting all the amiable attention, so make the most of this supremely sociable time by getting together with friends, neighbours or the folk you see every day and doing something you all enjoy. Let dull care wait until you're more in the mood!

Surrounding yourself with beautiful people or places will also appeal to you now, so grab any chance to escape your usual routine and visit beauty spots or lovely countryside. Visiting places with cultural connections, such as art galleries, might also be enjoyable, so steep yourself in all things lovely. It's also a good time to prettify your own neighbourhood, so why not investigate schemes and projects that will enhance your environment and improve your day-to-day dealings? You'll not only enjoy yourself but you might meet some interesting folk along the way.

If you're looking for love, you could find it's been on your doorstep all the time when you fall for a neighbour or cousin, meet a delectable darling through your daily dealings or are introduced to a special someone by a sibling. It's also a grand opportunity to show the folk you see everyday just how much they really mean to you, so don't be shy – open up your heart! And if you can't do it in person, don't hesitate to pick up the phone or put pen to paper. You might even hear something to your advantage in return!

VENUS IN YOUR FOURTH HOUSE

Home is where your heart is now, for you've got an overpowering need to be amongst your clan and know that you're loved, adored and appreciated. Just wallowing in the comforts of your own abode will fill you with happiness, but this is such a convivial and congenial time that it would be a shame to be by yourself when you could be soaking up some sociable surroundings. Why not organise a big gathering of the clans or just throw open the doors of your dwelling to all the folk you hold dear? It's a smashing time for a family party or celebration, whether you've got an excuse or not!

Playing happy families with kith and kin will warm the cockles of your heart, and if you've had a contretemps with one of the clan, this is your chance to forgive and forget. What's more, if some of your relatives have had a rumpus or rift, you'll be able to pour oil on troubled waters.

Is your domestic domain looking dreary and drab? Then get out the paints and papers and turn the place into somewhere splendid, sumptuous and sybaritic. You're imbued with super taste now, but try not to get so carried away that you spend every penny you own or transform your abode into something out of the Arabian Nights! If the budget can't stretch that far, even changing the cushions or buying some new knick-knacks will make all the difference in the world. Golden memories and treasured keepsakes that remind you of the good old days are also dear to your heart at the moment.

There's just one thing to watch, and that's your stomach! Rich foods or too much gracious living could play havoc with your waistline and really upset your tum!

VENUS IN YOUR FIFTH HOUSE

Delightful, delicious, delectable and de-lovely! Love is everywhere, so make the very most of this pleasurable patch. You're surrounded by an auspicious aura of amour and affection, helping you to get on well with everyone you meet. You don't have to put on any airs and graces to win friends, either, for they'll like you best if you let your true personality and charisma shine through. Be yourself!

With the planet of love dwelling in the solar abode of love, it's hardly surprising that *affaires de coeur* are starred for success at the moment, and whether you've been together for more years than you care to remember or are just starting a smashing, starry-eyed romance, you'll certainly wear your heart on your sleeve. If you're all on your ownsome, this could be the time you meet the man or maiden of your dreams, but do beware of reading more into a situation than really exists or of falling in love with love.

Remember that love comes in many forms, and an artistic endeavour, creative concern, cuddly pet or wee child could provide all you need in the way of enrichment, happiness and satisfaction. You're also at the height of your creative capabilities now, so make the most of them in whichever way comes naturally. With a little effort you'll be astounded at what you can achieve!

The only fly in the ointment comes from your lack of willpower, for you're not in the mood for hard work and want only to indulge in all the pleasures that life's got to offer. Well, why not? Trips to the theatre or cinema, evenings out, treats and sociable settings are just what the doctor ordered, so seek out enjoyment and entertainment and do yourself a power of good!

VENUS IN YOUR SIXTH HOUSE

Whistle while you work! Whatever you do in your workaday world, you'll really enjoy yourself now. What's more, your working conditions will be convivial and conducive, especially if you add tiny touches of your own with flowers, potted plants or even some of your favourite ornaments to brighten the place up. The more amenable and attractive your surroundings, the better you'll fare.

If you've fallen out with a client or colleague recently, grab this chance to make amends, talk things through and discover what's really wrong. Maybe you feel let down or disappointed with each other, but are too shy to say so? Well, speak up now so you can enjoy your renewed understanding of one another.

Dealings with all the folk you meet through your day-to-day doings should go well now, and it's a terrific time for a works outing, office party or knees-up with your colleagues. Artistic and creative pursuits will attract the attention of bosses and superiors, and a wee windfall might even come your way in the shape of an unexpected bonus, pay rise or perk. If someone new has joined your firm or factory, make 'em feel welcome and at home. Who knows, it could even turn into something special and be the start of anything from a firm friendship to a ravishing romance!

Even so, things may not be all plain sailing now, for Venus is the planet of leisure and pleasure whilst the sixth house rules work and being of service to others. That could mean your social life has to take a back seat when duty calls! As for your health, try not to overdo the good life, especially if you pulled out all the stops when Venus was in the fifth house. Fancy going on a diet?

VENUS IN YOUR SEVENTH HOUSE

Are those wedding bells I hear? Partnerships of all persuasions are looking luscious at the moment, and if you've been a single soul, this could be when you become one half of a contented couple, whether professional, platonic or provocatively passionate. What a time for making whoopee! Long-standing liaisons will also go from strength to strength now, for you'll be able to express your affections and feelings more clearly than usual and just enjoy each other's company in all sorts of wonderful ways. If your relationship has been racked with rows, recriminations or rifts, or a frosty and frigid feeling has developed between you, this is your chance to make amends, talk through your differences and try again. Put your ego on the back burner, don't be afraid to say you're sorry – and don't be surprised if you fall in love with each other all over again!

One thing's for sure – you need the comfort of companionship and the reassurance of knowing you're loved and cared for now, whether through wooing words, ardent actions or devoted deeds, but don't forget that dear ones will also want to know how you feel about *them*! If you've loved an amour from afar and want to declare your devotion, now's the time to speak up! Go on, be brave! Even if you and your other half are more like Darby and Joan than Romeo and Juliet, that's no reason not to say how much you mean to each other, especially if you usually take one another for granted.

Even business relationships will grow and prosper now, helped along by your current ability to tune into the feelings of others. Keep up the good work!

VENUS IN YOUR EIGHTH HOUSE

Pungent passions, fervent feelings and exotic emotions are on your amorous agenda at the moment, imbuing all encounters and intimate affairs with increased intensity and a stronger significance than usual. What's more, your libido's on the rise, making you long to increase your passion ration and let loose all your lusty, sensual and erotic urges and surges. Talk about hot stuff – you're burning with desire now, and could be bowled over by lust for a very sexy and salacious soul indeed! In fact, you just can't have love without lust at the moment, but beware of confusing the two or thinking you've fallen in love with a new amour when really you're after something very different indeed! Any new relationship that begins now will have a profound and intense impact on your life, no matter how short or long it turns out to be.

It's certainly a torrid time, but if you're part of a permanent pairing, don't let your partner think that you're interested only in their body and not their brain. Another possible problem is being tempted to trade off your sexual favours for mercenary or Machiavellian motives. Be warned that they'll soon backfire on you.

Financial matters are also to the fore now, especially where shared affairs or official and OHMS dealings are concerned. A wee windfall could come your way courtesy of the generosity of your other half, or an insurance policy, inheritance or endowment might pay up. You could also be tempted to go on a super spending spree at the moment, but take care you don't spend your partner's money or run up a big bill on a joint account!

VENUS IN YOUR NINTH HOUSE

Super duper! It's your love for the world around you that's being awakened now, broadening your mental and physical horizons and encouraging you to explore the serious and spiritual sides of life. Travelling to faraway places will be ultra-enjoyable now, especially if you visit somewhere you've never been before that's got a historical, philosophical or cultural connection. Beauty spots closer to home will also appeal, so grab every opportunity to surround yourself with visual delights!

It's a grand time for a pleasure trip, and you might even have a holiday romance that truly puts the cheery cherry on your cosmopolitan cake! Even if you stay at home, you could fall for someone from another clime, creed or culture, or even marry a sweetheart who takes you away from the country of your birth, for you're interested in people and places that are just that wee bit different now. There's definitely an international flavour in the air that'll spice up all your dealings!

Developments in a loving liaison could increase your insight and understanding of your relationship, or perhaps your amour will introduce you to new and exciting experiences and encounters?

Anything connected with religion, philosophy, metaphysics, further education, ecology and the environment will interest you and might even prove to be the beginning of a lifelong involvement.

Want to increase your brainpower? Then sign up for an evening class or further education course, especially if it's got artistic overtones, for who knows who you might meet along the way?

VENUS IN YOUR TENTH HOUSE

Vocational Venus! People in power and other influential folk are smiling favourably on you at the moment, so cash in on your attributes whilst this fortuitous phase lasts! Not only will you get on better with parents, senior citizens, mentors and father figures, but any dealings with managers, magnates or moguls will also go well. In fact, people in power or authority will be impressed by your current ability to get on well with everyone around you, ensuring a happy and harmonious atmosphere in your working world. It's a grand time to conduct negotiations or business dealings with bigwigs or the top brass, for you'll be able to put your case and state your terms without sounding unduly aggressive or argumentative. Mixing business with pleasure is another good idea!

Play your cards right now and success could be yours, due to the strength of your dazzling personality, smart appearance or artistic gifts. In fact, whatever you do for a living, your job could call on your creativity now and bring out all sorts of talents and skills you never knew you had!

If love enters your life, you may fall for someone who comes from a different social strata to yours, or who is way above you in other areas. There might even be a big age gap between you but don't worry, for it'll work in your favour! All the same, you should watch out for feelings of amour with ambitious or opportunist overtones, for that might make you set your cap at a boss, bigwig or someone who's loaded with loot, just for what you can get out of the liaison. Even if you're not aware of your mercenary machinations, once they're revealed they could ruin the relationship.

VENUS IN YOUR ELEVENTH HOUSE

Friendship, friendship, that's the perfect friendship, so don't keep yourself to yourself! Gregarious gatherings, social scenarios, group get-togethers and noisy neighbourly natterings will all be highly enjoyable at the moment, for you're feeling convivial and congenial, and in the mood for mixing and mingling as much as possible. In fact, you're such a sociable soul right now that you'll even be able to put up with people who usually bore you stiff or make you see red.

This is also your chance to meet all sorts of fresh and fascinating folk and widen your circle of acquaintances. If you've just moved to pastures new and are feeling left out or lonely, start chatting to the people next door, join a club or social group or find a hobby that'll be your passport to meeting personable people. Not only may you make some mates, but you might even meet that special someone you've been searching for all your life!

Business dealings, group activities and meetings will also do well now, and you'll enjoy feeling part of a team that's all pulling together. You'll also be able to put your own ego on the back burner whilst other people hog all the limelight.

Been cherishing a particular hope or dream? Then you'll adore throwing yourself into the swing of things now so that you can get your plans and projects off the ground and into action. A revelation could also come your way when you realise that a person who's been a pal is also the love of your life, or perhaps that your other half is also your best friend. What a turn-up for the books!

VENUS IN YOUR TWELFTH HOUSE

A radiant ring of ravishing romance surrounds you now, endowing all your emotions with a very nebulous, nectarine and even naive flavour. Amour may take a supremely spiritual and selfless turn when you have to give up something important for a loved one or devote yourself to looking after one who'll depend on you body and soul. That's all very well if you honestly don't mind all the effort and sacrifices involved, but beware of shouldering responsibilities without really thinking through what they will mean. Make sure you're acting from the best of motives, and don't confuse self-sacrifice with playing the put-upon martyr. Pretending you're Joan of Arc will do more harm than good, so don't even try!

Charitable or voluntary ventures may also involve you now, especially if you've got to roll up your sleeves and help out in some way. How about using your terrific talents to bake cakes or make some pretty presents, or maybe you'd like to rattle a collecting tin for your favourite good cause? Dealings with institutions, hospitals, prisons and the like could also be to the fore now, and although you might not enjoy any visits you have to make, they'll fill you with a strong sense of satisfaction in having put someone else's needs before your own.

A love affair that starts now will have all the makings of a fairy-tale romance, but don't read more into it than really exists or think that you've kissed a prince or princess only to see them turn back into a frog! Self-deception may be rife now. You could also begin an affair and have to keep it very hush-hush indeed – you'll love every minute of it!

HOW MUCH GET-UP AND GO
HAS MARTIAL MARS GIVEN YOU?

Are you always full of beans and raring to go, or would you rather
watch someone else doing all the hard work whilst you put your feet
up and take things easy? Well, whatever your answer, it's all due to
the placing of motivated Mars in your personal horoscope. Want to
know more? Then read on!

All the planets play an important role in our lives, and Mars is no
exception. Although smaller than the Earth, with a diameter of only
4,200 miles, mighty Mars exerts a considerable influence over us
astrologically. He represents our energy, aggression, sexual drive
and therefore the masculine instinct in both sexes, whilst Venus is
the feminine planet. When he is well-placed in a birth chart, Mars
can denote abundant energy, dynamism, pioneering spirit and a
lively nature, but a poor placing can mean aggression, selfishness,
brutality, rudeness and a hasty approach to life. The position of
Mars in a birth chart can also tell an astrologer volumes about that
person's sexuality.

As you will see from the charts, Mars takes approximately two
and a half years to complete his journey through all twelve signs, but
he can get up to some very odd things along the way. Sometimes
he'll dash through several signs like greased lightning, and then take
months to meander slowly through the next one. Every now and

then he even appears to travel backwards into the previous sign (what astrologers call 'turning retrograde') before moving forward again (or 'turning direct', in astrological parlance).

The charts on the next few pages list all the positions of Mars from January 1910 until December 1993. The numbers refer to the dates when Mars moves into a new sign, and the symbols refer to the sign that Mars is entering. To discover Mars's position on the day you were born, look down the chart until you find the year of your birth, then look across the top column until you find the right month. The square where the year and the month meet will give you Mars's position. For example, if you were born on 6 March 1923, you would have Mars in Taurus, because the chart tells you that Mars entered Taurus on 4 March. If you were born on 26 May 1963, on the other hand, you'll find a blank square, so you have to look back through the months until you find Mars's last movement. That was on 12 October 1962 when Mars entered Leo, and so that is the sign Mars occupied when you were born.

You probably know the symbols for the Sun signs, but I've listed them here just in case.

    ♈ Aries
    ♉ Taurus
    ♊ Gemini
    ♋ Cancer
    ♌ Leo
    ♍ Virgo
    ♎ Libra
    ♏ Scorpio
    ♐ Sagittarius
    ♑ Capricorn
    ♒ Aquarius
    ♓ Pisces

    ℞ Retrograde
    D Direct

GET UP AND GO WITH MARTIAL MARS

	JAN	FEB	MAR	APRIL	MAY	JUNE	JULY	AUG	SEPT	OCT	NOV	DEC
1910	23 ♉		14 ♊		2 ♋	19 ♌		6 ♏	22 ♎		7 ♐	21 ♐
1911		1 ♑	14 ♒	23 ♓		3 ♈	16 ♉		6 ♊		30 ♉ Rx	
1912	31 ♊ D		5 ♋	28 ♌			17 ♏		3 ♎	18 ♐	30 ♐	
1913	11 ♑	19 ♒	30 ♓		8 ♈	17 ♉	29 ♊		16 ♋			
1914					2 ♌	26 ♏		15 ♎	29 ♐		11 ♐	22 ♑
1915	30 ♒		10 ♓	17 ♈	26 ♉		6 ♊	19 ♋		8 ♌		
1916					29 ♏		23 ♎		9 ♐	22 ♐		2 ♑
1917	10 ♒	17 ♓	27 ♈		5 ♉	15 ♊	28 ♋		12 ♌		2 ♏	
1918	11 ♎	26 ♏ Rx				24 ♎ D		17 ♐		1 ♐	11 ♑	20 ♒
1919	27 ♓		7 ♈	15 ♉	26 ♊		9 ♋	23 ♌		10 ♏		1 ♎
1920		1 ♐		24 ♎ Rx			11 ♐ D		5 ♐	19 ♑	28 ♒	
1921	5 ♓	13 ♈	25 ♉		6 ♊	19 ♋		3 ♌	19 ♏		7 ♎	26 ♐
1922		19 ♐						14 ♑		31 ♒		12 ♓
1923	21 ♈		4 ♉	16 ♊	31 ♋		16 ♌		1 ♏	18 ♎		4 ♐
1924	20 ♐		7 ♑	25 ♒		25 ♓		25 ♒ Rx		20 ♓ D		19 ♈
1925		5 ♉	24 ♊		10 ♋	26 ♌		13 ♏	29 ♎		14 ♐	28 ♐
1926		9 ♑	23 ♒		4 ♓	15 ♈		1 ♉				

GET UP AND GO WITH MARTIAL MARS

	JAN	FEB	MAR	APRIL	MAY	JUNE	JULY	AUG	SEPT	OCT	NOV	DEC
1927		22 ♊		17 ♋		6 ♌	25 ♍		11 ♎	26 ♏		8 ♐
1928	19 ♑	28 ♒		8 ♓	17 ♈	26 ♉		9 ♊		3 ♋		20 ♊ Rx
1929			11 ♋ D		13 ♌		4 ♍	22 ♎		7 ♏	19 ♐	29 ♑
1930		7 ♒	17 ♓	25 ♈		3 ♉	15 ♊	28 ♋		21 ♌		
1931		17 ♋ Rx	30 ♌ D			11 ♍		2 ♎	17 ♏	31 ♐		10 ♑
1932	18 ♒	25 ♓		3 ♈	12 ♉	22 ♊		5 ♋	21 ♌		14 ♍	
1933							7 ♎	26 ♏		9 ♐	19 ♑	28 ♒
1934		4 ♓	14 ♈	23 ♉		3 ♊	16 ♋	31 ♌		18 ♍		11 ♎
1935							30 ♏		17 ♐	29 ♑		7 ♒
1936	15 ♓	22 ♈		2 ♉	13 ♊	26 ♋		10 ♌	27 ♍		15 ♎	
1937	6 ♏		13 ♐		15 ♏ Rx			9 ♐ D	30 ♑		12 ♒	22 ♓
1938	31 ♈		12 ♉	24 ♊		7 ♋	23 ♌		8 ♍	25 ♎		12 ♏
1939	29 ♐		21 ♑		25 ♒		22 ♑ Rx		24 ♒ D		20 ♓	
1940	4 ♈	17 ♉		2 ♊	18 ♋		3 ♌	20 ♍		6 ♎	21 ♏	
1941	5 ♐	18 ♑		2 ♒	16 ♓		2 ♈					
1942	12 ♉		7 ♊	26 ♋		14 ♌		1 ♍	17 ♎		2 ♏	16 ♐
1943	27 ♑		9 ♒	17 ♓	27 ♈		8 ♉	24 ♊				

56

GET UP AND GO WITH MARTIAL MARS

	JAN	FEB	MAR	APRIL	MAY	JUNE	JULY	AUG	SEPT	OCT	NOV	DEC
1944			28 ♋		23 ♌		12 ♍	29 ♎		14 ♏	26 ♐	
1945	6 ♑	14 ♒	25 ♓		3 ♈	11 ♉	23 ♊		8 ♋		12 ♌	27 ♋ Rx
1946				23 ♌ D		20 ♍		10 ♎	25 ♏		7 ♐	17 ♑
1947	25 ♒		5 ♓	12 ♈	21 ♉		1 ♊	14 ♋		1 ♌		1 ♍
1948		12 ♌ Rx			19 ♍ D		17 ♎		4 ♏	17 ♐	27 ♑	
1949	5 ♒	12 ♓	22 ♈	30 ♉		10 ♊	23 ♋		7 ♌	27 ♍		26 ♎
1950			28 ♏ Rx			12 ♎ D		11 ♏	26 ♐		6 ♑	15 ♒
1951	23 ♓		2 ♈	10 ♉	22 ♊		4 ♋	18 ♌		5 ♍	24 ♎	
1952	20 ♍							28 ♐		12 ♑	22 ♒	31 ♓
1953		8 ♈	20 ♉		1 ♊	14 ♋	30 ♌		15 ♍		2 ♎	20 ♍
1954		10 ♐		13 ♑			3 ♐ Rx	25 ♑ D		22 ♒		4 ♓
1955	15 ♈	26 ♉		11 ♊	26 ♋		11 ♌	27 ♍		13 ♎	29 ♏	
1956	14 ♐	29 ♑		15 ♒		3 ♓						6 ♈
1957	29 ♉		18 ♊		5 ♋	22 ♌		8 ♍	24 ♎		9 ♏	23 ♐
1958		4 ♑	17 ♒	27 ♓		7 ♈	21 ♉		21 ♊	29 ♉ Rx		
1959		11 ♊ D		10 ♋		1 ♌	20 ♍		6 ♎	21 ♏		4 ♐
1960	14 ♑	23 ♒		2 ♓	11 ♈	20 ♉		2 ♊	21 ♋			

57

GET UP AND GO WITH MARTIAL MARS

	JAN	FEB	MAR	APRIL	MAY	JUNE	JULY	AUG	SEPT	OCT	NOV	DEC
1961		5 ♊ Rx 7 ♋ D			6 ♌	29 ♍		17 ♎		2 ♏	14 ♐	25 ♑
1962		2 ♒	12 ♓	20 ♈	29 ♉		9 ♊	22 ♋		12 ♌		
1963	·.					3 ♍	27 ♎		12 ♏	26 ♐		5 ♑
1964	13 ♒	20 ♓	29 ♈		8 ♉	17 ♊	31 ♋		15 ♌		6 ♍	
1965						29 ♎		21 ♏		4 ♐	14 ♑	23 ♒
1966	30 ♓		10 ♈	18 ♉	29 ♊		11 ♋	26 ♌		13 ♍		4 ♎
1967		13 ♏	31 ♎ Rx				20 ♍ D		10 ♐	23 ♑		2 ♒
1968	9 ♓	17 ♈	28 ♉		9 ♊	21 ♋		6 ♌	22 ♍		9 ♎	30 ♏
1969		25 ♐							21 ♑		5 ♒	16 ♓
1970	25 ♈		7 ♉	19 ♊		2 ♋	18 ♌		3 ♍	20 ♎		7 ♏
1971	23 ♐		12 ♑		4 ♒						7 ♓	27 ♈
1972		11 ♉	27 ♊		13 ♋	29 ♌		15 ♍		1 ♎	16 ♏	31 ♐
1973		12 ♑	27 ♒		8 ♓	21 ♈		13 ♉		30 ♈ Rx		24 ♉ D
1974		27 ♊	20 ♋			9 ♌	28 ♍		13 ♎	28 ♏		11 ♐
1975	22 ♑		3 ♒	12 ♓	21 ♈		1 ♉	15 ♊		17 ♋	26 ♊ Rx	
1976			19 ♋ D		16 ♌		7 ♍	24 ♎		9 ♏	21 ♐	
1977	1 ♑	9 ♒	20 ♓	28 ♈		6 ♉	18 ♊		1 ♋	27 ♌		

58

GET UP AND GO WITH MARTIAL MARS

	JAN	FEB	MAR	APRIL	MAY	JUNE	JULY	AUG	SEPT	OCT	NOV	DEC
1978	26 ♋ Rx			11 ♌ D		14 ♍		4 ♎	20 ♏		2 ♐	13 ♑
1979	21 ♒	28 ♓		7 ♈	16 ♉	26 ♊		9 ♋	25 ♌		20 ♍	
1980			12 ♌ Rx		4 ♍ D		11 ♎	29 ♏		12 ♐	22 ♑	31 ♒
1981		7 ♓	17 ♈	25 ♉		5 ♊	18 ♋		2 ♌	21 ♍		16 ♎
1982								3 ♏	20 ♐		1 ♑	10 ♒
1983	18 ♓	25 ♈		6 ♉	17 ♊	29 ♋		14 ♌	30 ♍		18 ♎	
1984	11 ♏							18 ♐		5 ♑	16 ♒	25 ♓
1985		3 ♈	15 ♉	26 ♊		9 ♋	25 ♌		10 ♍	28 ♎		15 ♏
1986		2 ♐	28 ♑							9 ♒	26 ♓	
1987	9 ♈	21 ♉		6 ♊	21 ♋		7 ♌	23 ♍		9 ♎	24 ♏	
1988	9 ♐	22 ♑		6 ♒	22 ♓		14 ♈			24 ♓ Rx	2 ♈ D	
1989	19 ♉		11 ♊	29 ♋		17 ♌		4 ♍	20 ♎		4 ♏	18 ♐
1990	30 ♑		12 ♒	21 ♓	31 ♈		13 ♉	31 ♊			14 ♉ Rx	
1991	21 ♊ D			3 ♋	27 ♌		16 ♍		1 ♎	17 ♏	29 ♐	
1992	9 ♑	18 ♒	28 ♓		6 ♈	15 ♉	27 ♊		12 ♋			
1993				28 ♌		23 ♍		12 ♎	27 ♏		9 ♐	20 ♑

MARS IN ARIES

Aries is one of the two signs ruled by Mars, so there's no doubt this is a very powerful placing indeed. In fact, even if you haven't got the Sun in Aries you will have plenty of Arien traits. For example, you exude energy, enterprise and enthusiasm from every pore, and often infect everyone around you with your very own brand of get-up-and-go. You're also imbued with an adventurous and competitive spirit, and need to be first at everything you do. That can also make you a wee bit selfish, for you usually put your own needs first and other people's a very poor second. When it comes to sexual set-ups, you're supremely lusty, libidinous and lascivious, but you have to put your fervent feelings into ardent action – platonic pairings are not for you! Healthwise, you suffer from headaches and can be accident prone. You've probably got a quick temper, but channelling your fury into physical activities will help you work off steam and also keep the peace!

MARS IN TAURUS

It takes a lot to make you lose your temper, but once you're angry there's no mistaking it! In fact, it's a case of lighting the blue touch paper and standing well back! Try to deal with problems as they arise instead of bottling up your feelings until you've just got to let them out, for that way you'll avoid all sorts of unpleasant scenes. If you were born with the Sun in Taurus, Leo, Scorpio or Aquarius, this placing will increase your innate obstinacy and make you very stubborn indeed. Either way, you're steadfast, sure of your beliefs and confident in the courage of your convictions. You aren't frightened of hard work either, though you can get stuck in a dreary rut or insist on adhering to a rigid routine. Emotional and financial security are of prime importance to you, and so is a healthy and happy sex life. Your throat may well be your weak spot when it comes to health, so take good care of it!

MARS IN GEMINI

Mars is a planet associated with energetic pursuits, but you probably prefer curling up with a good book to dashing about like a dervish! If that's the case, try to find some way of letting off steam every now and then, because otherwise all your pent-up energy will be turned towards spats, squabbles and some of your sarcastic comments. You'll also find fault with yourself which will only make matters worse. Frittering away your time, abandoning projects halfway through or doing too many things at once so that you end up achieving very little are all dangers with this placing. Instead, try to channel your efforts in definite directions so you can feel proud of yourself, and not angry. When it comes to close encounters of the sexy kind, you believe variety is the spice of life. Partners with a tired old technique will get short shrift from you! Look after your hands and arms, for you can easily burn or cut them.

MARS IN CANCER

Talk about tenacious! You really stick to your guns, following projects through from beginning to end. No wonder you're such an impressive person to have around! Loved ones are also aware of your sticking power, but that's often where the problems start, for sometimes you just don't know when to let go. The VIPs of your heart can bask in the warmth of your love, but there are times when they feel they're being smothered by your claustrophobic caring. Try not to come on so strong and you'll soon see what a difference it makes! Sexually speaking, you're a supremely sensual and tremendously tender amour, with an intuition that tells you what your other half needs. Your temper's on a very short, sharp fuse, and your natural tendency to bottle problems up only makes matters worse, You've also got a marvellous memory, which means you never forget a hurt or slight and aren't shy of saying so. You must learn to let go a little!

MARS IN LEO

You're blessed with a real love of life, helped out by a delicious dollop of energy, enthusiasm and *joie de vivre*. Making other people happy makes you happy too, so it's not surprising you're high on everyone's popularity polls, especially when it comes to amorous activities! In fact, your natural sense of drama means you stand out from the crowd, though sometimes it can backfire by making you a show-off or a mite too full of your own importance. You can also be a bit bombastic or ride roughshod over folk who aren't able to stand up for themselves. Artistic and creative concerns see you really in your element whether you're making the most of your own talents or appreciating those of other people. Combining exercise and artistry is a wonderful way to improve your health, so anything connected with dancing should be right up your street. Look after your back, though, as it's easily strained.

MARS IN VIRGO

Opposite forces are at work here, for although Mars is a planet of assertion and aggression, Virgo is a sign that's shy, modest and prefers to take a back seat. As a result, this placing can make you unsure of yourself or even doubtful of your own abilities. Even so, you're marvellously methodical and a tower of strength when it comes to work, for you'll gladly get on with the job in hand and do it to the very best of your ability. Be sure, though, to avoid getting too bogged down in detail and try to take an overall view whenever possible. Healthwise, it's your nerves that are affected by this placing, making you edgy, highly strung and unable to relax. All that can lead to a host of ailments caused by tension, so try to burn off your nervous energy before it gets the better of you. Your sex life can also suffer, for unless you were born under an emotional Water sign or an enthusiastic Fire sign, you could find it hard to express your emotions or perhaps you feel sex is much too messy for you!

MARS IN LIBRA

Partnerships are of paramount importance to you, especially when they make the most of your stunning sexuality. In fact, you're a real romantic who likes to make your feelings felt in a very physical fashion! That can mean you fall in love with love, place your partner on an idealistic pedestal or believe they can do no wrong. As a result, you're all set for a broken heart when you discover your idealised inamorata has feet of clay after all. It can be hard for you to learn the lessons of love, for you seem to repeat the same romantic mistakes over and over again! When it comes to the energetic side of Mars, you veer between enthusiastic exercise on one hand and complete lethargy when you just can't be bothered to make any effort at all on the other. Anyone who irritates you will spark off your quick temper, and you could suffer from headaches or kidney problems. Taking a little steady exercise might make all the difference, you know!

MARS IN SCORPIO

Well, there are no half measures for you! Along with Pluto, Mars is one of the two rulers of Scorpio, so this is a particularly powerful planetary placing. Your emotions are immense, intense and complex, making you very highly charged. You may not always show your feelings but that doesn't mean they don't exist. In fact, your still waters run very deep indeed! A satisfying sex life spells the difference between happiness and heartache, for you've an over-powering need to express your emotions through your intimate affairs, and any blockages or barriers could lead to obsessive ideas or compulsive emotions. Another pitfall to watch is becoming jealous, possessive or envious towards your loved ones, or suspecting them of letting you down. When you lose your temper it's like an atomic bomb going off, and you certainly leave folk in no doubt about your furious feelings!

MARS IN SAGITTARIUS

Full of beans, you're a real live wire and a bundle of energy. In fact, you find it hard to sit still for long, because as far as you're concerned, relaxation leads to restlessness. Anything that smacks of a challenge is right up your street, for you hate life when it's hum-drum, dreary and predictable. Instead, you love to rise to the occasion and live on your wits, because it makes you feel alive and in the driving seat. A possible problem is that you sometimes think the grass is greener on the other side of the fence, and so you keep switching projects, jobs or even homes in a continual effort to improve your lot. You can also flit from one project to another and then back again before giving both of them up and starting on something else that seems more exciting! When you look for an amour you're just as interested in their brain as their body, for you want someone whose intellectual abilities match your own and who shares your need for fervent but fun-filled sex. Happy hunting!

MARS IN CAPRICORN

Mars is associated with competitiveness and the need to come first, and when he falls in Capricorn the result is a placing where career and ambition are of prime importance. Status, honour and prestige all mean a lot to you, whether you want to become a captain of industry or the head of a local society or organisation. In fact, whatever you do for a living and no matter how humble or high-falutin your background, you're determined to improve your lot, even at the expense of your family or a happy love life, because your innate ambition can turn you into a real workaholic who never knows when to stop. Even so, your powers of endurance are second to none, and you can put up with all sorts of hardships and problems that would leave other folk standing. Take care of your joints and bones, as they're your weak spots. As for the sexual stakes, you can be a wee bit chilly at first, but when you're with the perfect paramour you soon get into your stride!

MARS IN AQUARIUS

What a whacky person you are! Your friends (and you're bound to have lots of 'em) enjoy your entertaining, eccentric and erratic ways, for they never know what you're going to do next. Rather than follow the crowd, you prefer to strike out on your own, making the most of your originality and unique personality. You're vibrating with vim and vitality, so make the most of them through any sporting or athletic activity that appeals to you, as otherwise they could surface in all sorts of tension, angst and anger. Circulatory problems can also plague you, especially in cold weather, so you need to take plenty of exercise. You can also be more than a wee bit stubborn for once you've made up your mind nothing and no one can change it! Your humanitarian spirit is never far away, making you eager to help others whether you know them or not. When it comes to amour, your innate independence and restlessness may mean that you enjoy experimenting with sex but don't want to be tied down to one person.

MARS IN PISCES

Fountains of fervent feelings and cascades of considerable caring gush out of you like water from a tap, making it important that you channel such sensitivity and imagination in the right directions. There's no doubt that sex means a lot to you, for it's a wonderful way of showing loved ones how you feel and it also makes the most of your superbly sensual and voluptuous talents. Even so, you could easily sacrifice your love life for a vocation or calling that involves helping others. On the other hand, perhaps you're unable to view a loving liaison in its true light, instead imbuing it with all sorts of qualities and strengths that don't really exist? If so, you should steer clear of drink and drugs, for they'll do you no good at all. Activities such as swimming, skating, dancing or yoga are ideal for you, as they provide plenty of exercise without being too tiring.

RUSSELL'S SUN SIGN TRAVEL GUIDE

SUN SIGNS	TOWNS AND CITIES	COUNTRIES
Aries	Birmingham, Brunswick, Capua, Florence, Krakow, Leicester, Marseilles, Naples, Utrecht, Verona	Argentina, Denmark, England, France, Germany, Iran, Poland, Syria, Zimbabwe
Taurus	Dublin, Eastbourne, Hastings, Leipzig, Lucerne, Mantua, Palermo, Parma, St Louis	Afghanistan, Austria, Capri, Cyprus, Greek Islands, Iran, Ireland, Ischia, Israel, Japan, Norway, Switzerland
Gemini	Bruges, Cardiff, Cordoba, London, Melbourne, Metz, New York, Nuremburg, Plymouth, San Francisco, Versailles	Armenia, Belgium, Denmark, Egypt, Jordan, Sardinia, South Africa, USA, Wales

Cancer — Algiers, Amsterdam, Berne, Cadiz, Genoa, Istanbul, Magdeburg, Manchester, Milan, New York, Stockholm, Tokyo, Tunis, Venice, York — Algeria, Canada, Holland, New Zealand, North and West Africa, Paraguay, Scotland

Leo — Bath, Bristol, Bombay, Chicago, Damascus, Los Angeles, Madrid, Philadelphia, Portsmouth, Prague, Rome, Syracuse — Chad, Cyprus, Czechoslovakia, Italy, Jamaica, Lebanon, Romania, Sicily, Southern Iraq, South of France, Spain

Virgo — Athens, Boston, Corinth, Heidelberg, Jerusalem, Lyons, State of Virginia, Paris, Reading, most spas and health resorts — Belize, Brazil, Bulgaria, Crete, Greece, Lower Silesia, Mesopotamia, Turkey, West Indies, USA, Yugoslavia

Libra — Antwerp, Copenhagen, Freiburg, Frankfurt, Johannesburg, Leeds, Lisbon, Nottingham, Vienna — Alsace, Argentina, Austria, Burma, Canada, China, France, Indochina, Japan, New Zealand, some South Pacific Islands, Tibet, Upper Egypt

Scorpio — Baltimore, Cincinnati, Dover, Fez, Hull, Halifax, Liverpool, Milwaukee, Newcastle-upon-Tyne, New Orleans, St John's (Newfoundland), Stockport, Valencia, Washington DC — Algeria, Bavaria, Korea, Morocco, Norway, Poland, Syria, the Transvaal, Uruguay, USSR

Sagittarius	Avignon, Bradford, Budapest, Cologne, Naples, Nottingham, Sheffield, Stuttgart, Toledo, Toronto	Arabia, Australia, Hungary, Kenya, South Africa, Spain, Yugoslavia, Zaire
Capricorn	Brussels, Constanta, Delhi, Ghent, Oxford, Mecklenburg, Mexico City, Port Said, the administrative or bureaucratic centres of capital cities	Afghanistan, Albania, Bulgaria, Cuba, India, Lithuania, Mexico, the Orkneys, Saudi Arabia, Saxony, the Shetland Isles, Sweden
Aquarius	Bremen, Hamburg, Moscow, Salzberg, St Petersburg	Ethiopia, Hungary, India, Iran, Israel, Poland, Sweden, USSR, Yugoslavia
Pisces	Alexandria, Bournemouth, Compostella, Jerusalem, Seville, Warsaw	Brazil, Gobi Desert, many small Mediterranean islands, Pakistan, Portugal, the Sahara, Scandinavia

THE TRADITIONS OF ASTROLOGY

SIGN	NOs	COLOUR	DAY	STONE	METAL	FLOWER	BODY AREA
Aries	1	Red	Tuesday	Diamond	Iron	Geranium	Head
Taurus	2	Copper, dark blue	Friday	Emerald	Copper	Daisy	Throat
Gemini	3	Yellows	Wednesday	Agate, garnet	Mercury	Daffodil	Hands, chest
Cancer	4	Pearl, silver	Monday	Pearl	Silver	White rose, lily	Breast
Leo	5	Amber, gold	Sunday	Ruby	Gold	Sunflower	Heart, spine
Virgo	6	Autumnal shades	Wednesday	Peridot	Mercury	Lily of the valley	Intestines
Libra	7	Pastel blues and pinks	Friday	Sapphire	Copper	Rose	Kidneys
Scorpio	8	Black, burgundy	Tuesday	Opal	Iron	Dahlia, rhododendron	Sexual organs
Sagittarius	9	Imperial purple	Thursday	Topaz	Tin	Delphinium	Thighs, hips
Capricorn	10, 1	Black, grey, white	Saturday	Turquoise	Lead	Pansy	Shins, knees
Aquarius	11, 2	Turquoise, blues	Saturday	Amethyst	Lead	Crocus, snowdrop	Ankles
Pisces	12, 3	Greens, sea blues	Thursday	Aquamarine	Tin	Poppy	Feet

WHAT 1993 HAS IN STORE
FOR YOUR
LOVE, CASH AND WORK

LOVE

It's true that Leo's personal relationships have been a troublesome area for some time past. The grim planet Saturn traversing your opposite sign of Aquarius has made you question many assumptions you previously held, although that in itself was no bad thing. Signs of getting back on to an even keel in the way your feel about the whole concept of commitment continue to be a feature of 1993. You are such a dramatic individualist that sometimes you find it difficult to take a partner's views and desires into consideration. In May, Saturn makes a grand entrance into Pisces, which in your solar chart is the area concerned with intimacy and sexual matters. This should be a golden opportunity for you to discuss your deepest feelings and desires with your partner. This can only strengthen your relationship, so have no fears that you will be judged harshly.

The whole area of your sex life is due for a boost when the fiery and passionate planet Mars muscles his way into your sign in April. Talk about volcanic passion! The entire sexual scenario is going to heat up quite a few degrees right through until June. Unattached Lions could well find that the partner of your dreams turns up at this time. Venus, the lovesome lady of the heavens, occupies your solar area of travel and deep thinking from February, so an attraction to a foreign-born individual or someone who has a wide-ranging philosophical nature is on the cards for you.

Leos are not happy unless you can indulge in a little innocent flirtation (sometimes it's not so innocent, you naughty thing!). The pre-Christmas period provides the perfect stage for you to woo your way through a swathe of bowled-over beaux or belles. You should really be in fine flirtatious form, making this a Noel to remember! Ever-active Mars endows you with ample energy to indulge your steamy and sensual nature to the full. If romantic dalliance is your thing, then 1993 should provide a truly passionate period. You're such a luscious Lion!

CASH

July is usually quite an expensive month for most Leos and 1993 will prove no exception. In fact, you have to wait until your ruler, the Sun, enters Virgo before you start to feel flush after the sometimes outrageous expenses of the holiday season. When Venus and Mercury also put in an appearance in the sign of the Virgin, the whole area of your finances will take on a much healthier look.

It must be admitted that partners will be a considerable drain on your resources for much of the year. This may not be their fault but, even so, you must guard against any feelings of resentment that their dependence might give rise to.

Saturn's brief visit to the sign of Pisces in May puts a spotlight on long-term investments, insurance, bank accounts and contracts of all kinds. It's in your nature to let the more boring pieces of paperwork go by the board until your attention is absolutely vital, but you should use this period to get your financial realities in some form of order. This reorganisation is long overdue, and before Saturn sidles out of this area in early July you should put your pecuniary house in order. The planet will return in 1994, so you can look on the period May–July as an advance notice of things to come. Practical monetary affairs deserve some serious attention.

From September onward you're entering a very productive and prosperous patch when it comes to earning a crust or improving your pecuniary position through the sweat of your brow. Stick to your principles over every issue that threatens your personal integrity and the fickle whims of fortune will lead you to prodigious profits. You're about to set a profound economic example to everyone around you.

In short, 1993 is not a time to let any of your slapdash inclinations lead you into the risky pathways of gambling away your hard-earned resources. You should stick to the straight and narrow as far as your pennies are concerned. Conserving your personal economy should be your aim, for ingenious budgeting is not as hard or as restrictive as it seems. You'll soon get the hang of it!

WORK

Leos have got a lot going for them in 1993. The ingenious and dynamic vibrations of the mingled rays of Uranus and Neptune really make this a year when you can cut corners and achieve great things in the professional stakes. Though some of the career pathways opening to you may be unconventional, you will derive immense satisfaction from not following the old well-worn pathways of day-to-day responsibilities. You are entering an extremely idealistic time in your life, so your attention could be drawn to doing something worthwhile for the community at large rather than concentrating on basically selfish interests. Your ideas are bound to be inspirational, so if you are at all involved in charity work, you can boost the finances of your chosen cause with consummate ease.

Saturn moves into a very sensitive corner of your solar chart from May, astrally enhancing your ability adroitly to handle the resources of others to the maximum advantage. Your chief problem in the active months ahead is keeping your mind on the job in hand, as playful pals and empty-headed acquaintances try their utmost to seduce you from the vocational straight and narrow. Seduction is the name of the game in the social scene too, with romantic allure wresting your mind from professional concerns. If you can get a word in edgeways, spell out your aims, ambitions and aspirations to your loved one in no uncertain terms and you'll be well set on the path of achievement.

Your autumnal astral array ushers in a more precise pecuniary phase. By then your plans should be polished and your professional strategies should be in order. It will do you no harm at all to combine business with pleasure as you woo your way through your contacts to your best advantage. The dramatic and charming side of the Leo nature should come in very handy in advancing your aims and proving to your peers that you are a force to be reckoned with.

YOUR DAY-BY-DAY-GUIDE TO 1993

JANUARY

FRIDAY, 1st. Happy New Year! All that festivity has got your wild nature fizzling on this first day of a brand-new annum. Powerful forces are pushing you forward, determined that this year will not be the same as the last. You'll relish any extra freedom now as a restless ray stirs up your more impatient and independent side. Trouble is, the thought of going back to the tiresome treadmill just makes you want to jack it all in and run away to sea. Satisfy your wanderlust with a thrilling travel book or a strenuous spot of sport, for there's really no need to take extreme action just yet.

SATURDAY, 2nd. The need for efficiency is occupying your thoughts as mini Mercury bolts briskly into your horoscopic house of work and service. You're a mental marvel at organising realistic rotas and productive programmes that will soon have your entire world shipshape and Bristol fashion. Working Lions will want to reorganise their place of employment but if you're looking for work, meetings and messages in the weeks ahead can do your cause the world of good.

SUNDAY, 3rd. Every kind of partnership in your life looks good now. Whether it's love and marriage or money and business, by using the delving rays around you now any heart-to-heart you have will create a solid and promising base for joint development in the future. There's a real understanding in all one-to-one dealings today. It's been ages since you've achieved such a wonderful rapport with both your partner in life and your colleagues in business affairs.

MONDAY, 4th. You're sitting firmly atop an emotional volcano this Monday and unless you face up to the fact that there's a family feud afoot, you'll have to cope with the explosive consequences. Your kith and kin are in the grip of unfounded suspicions that are fast becoming obsessions, but it'll do no good to treat their compulsive ideas with the contempt they deserve. It's up to you to defuse highly charged situations with understanding and a willingness to listen.

TUESDAY, 5th. With you it's a matter of honour to back your friends to the hilt if they're in any kind of trouble, so you won't hesitate to help a perplexed pal who appeals to you today. Troubles shared are troubles halved, and you'll benefit from knowing there's a bond formed between you now. You're keen to feel you belong to a group of your peers and may want to join a more formal society or club.

WEDNESDAY, 6th. It's January and your mood may be wintry to match as you gloomily contemplate the state of the world and the difficulties confronting anyone who wants to put it right. Your kind and compassionate soul wants to soothe and heal the ills of anyone who's suffering and you can make good progress so long as you don't expect too much of yourself. A partner offers valuable and perfectly practical support to help you on your way.

THURSDAY, 7th. With a delicate refinement and sympathetic sensitivity the tender rays of Madam Moon are mingled with those of voluptuous mistress Venus to bring you a magical day of delicious emotion and romance.. Take the opportunity to let a loved one know just how much you care and you'll be touched to discover what a difference it can make.

FRIDAY, 8th. If you want to make this more than just a fretful Friday, why not arrange a family reunion or at least decide to spend some time chewing the fat with any relatives within reach. There may not be any earth-shaking news to impart but you'll all benefit from the nice secure sense of belonging that results from simply keeping in touch. It doesn't take much to make your kith and kin happy, so why not make the first move?

SATURDAY, 9th. If you thought you had your workmates sussed, you'll be stunned today as they display an unsuspected side to their nature. Don't dig in your heels and hold out for the status quo in your workplace, for a revolution in the organisation of your day-to-day tasks could bring many benefits and plenty of excitement!

Healthwise, an alternative medicine or therapy could help a nagging ailment.

SUNDAY, 10th. It's a dodgy day when you'll be enticed into doing things you wouldn't usually consider, but the alluring and charming ways of a woman especially will pull a veil over reality and make you follow a line that is pure fantasy. Disillusionment could set in if you are compelled to toe the line today, and you'll need to be on your guard against any form of escapism, even if a harsh reality has to be faced.

MONDAY, 11th. Revelations made yesterday could leave you and your family feeling a little awkward with each other, as some things can never be quite the same again. That's no bad thing, but meantime you'll all need to be very discreet and diplomatic with each other whilst you form a sensitive and supportive structure for your entire clan. Don't try to force the pace.

TUESDAY, 12th. Even for an exuberant Lion you can be remarkably forward-looking at times, and today's stars will have you bursting with optimism and enthusiasm for your future plans. You're not willing to settle for second best, and why should you when you can see your way clear to going right to the top? You can lay plans now that will gain the support of your colleagues, so do take time to share your ideas and set up business meetings.

WEDNESDAY, 13th. Finances are looking much better today, although you mustn't expect miracles overnight. All kinds of money and financial matters connected with the home are particularly advantageous now. Look towards insurance or even possessions as the keys to future security. A little forethought now will save you no end of concern later. It's always better to be safe than sorry, and you'll feel much happier knowing that you are covered against any eventuality.

THURSDAY, 14th. Thursday's stars emphasise your most pragmatic and practical side, making it difficult for you to justify the

76

expense of extra little comforts or an evening spent out in the company of friends. It's not like you to count the pennies too closely – you're usually generosity itself. So before you apply the brakes to your extremely social nature, you'd better buck up your ideas or folk will accuse you of being a wet blanket!

FRIDAY, 15th. Your mind's overflowing with interesting and useful ideas these days, but there's a limit to the amount of input you can cope with and it could be you've already overstepped the mark. Your health will suffer if you begin to live on your nerves without adequate rest, relaxation and recreation, so take my timely tip and let the rat race pass you by for a wee while. There, that's better!

SATURDAY, 16th. If you're to achieve all you instinctively know you're capable of, there are certain working conditions, employment obstacles and fitness failings that must be eliminated. Whatever your goals may be, now's the time to work out precisely what's standing in your way in order to rid yourself of unnecessary handicaps. It'll be much easier than you suppose, so don't shirk any issues.

SUNDAY, 17th. Well, I'm glad to see that you've simmered down! In fact, you're on a completely even keel once more, ready to take the ups and downs of everyday life in your stride with barely a ripple in your equanimity. Friends and family will be so pleased with your good humour they'll be falling over themselves to lend a helping hand and that can only increase your general enjoyment of the day!

MONDAY, 18th. The dreary demands of duty and domestic obligations go by the board, as you're such a fun-loving Lion that you really can't be bothered to deal with anything as dull as the washing-up or fixing the fence. You feel so good and optimistic that your nearest and dearest won't mind too much, especially if you give in to your generous impulses and take them out to a slap-up meal. You have the luck of the devil today!

TUESDAY, 19th. There are times when your other half's dull and dreary down-to-earth attitude drives you to distraction, but not this Tuesday when you have good reason to be thankful for their constructive common sense. Professional partnerships are especially favoured by today's productive planets, as you supply the creative spark that gets the people you're working with motivated and moving. Teamwork produces terrific results now!

WEDNESDAY, 20th. Wednesday's a very important day, for your very own master the Sun swings into your solar house of relationships, shining a bright light of love on your one-to-one affairs. Anything from marriage to anniversaries or business cartels and partnerships is boosted now, making this a time to join forces with others to add power to your potential.

THURSDAY, 21st. Wee Mercury's entry into your horoscopic area of one-to-one partnerships helps you to communicate freely in your chosen relationships. Very often one-to-one affairs can break down because neither partner is aware of their loved one's needs. Bring your hidden worries and doubts into the open now and your other half will have a clue as to what you're wanting from them and vice versa. Marvellous Mercury manages a merciful mental rapport now!

FRIDAY, 22nd. Your relationships are twisted sharply into focus, thanks to the Aquarian New Moon today. You can't hide or deceive yourself over anything that's wrong with your one-to-one affairs – you have a chance to get the best out of your partnerships but it means coming to terms with the realisation that you must look at your other half in a new light, for both your sakes.

SATURDAY, 23rd. Are there sensitive subjects you and your partner just don't talk about, or topics too temperamental to touch on? Don't put up with the limitations this places on your partnership, for communication lies at the heart of any relationship, whether it's romantically oriented or business based. Have a heart-to-heart with

78

anyone close to you now, as you have the verbal skills required to put your true feelings into words.

SUNDAY, 24th. Is your partner plotting behind your back or simply lying doggo about an intimate matter that would be better out in the open? You're a supersleuth today and with a little determination can winkle out the most subtle of secrets in your private world. Take care that you don't dig up a hornets' nest that would have been better left alone, though!

MONDAY, 25th. Intimate matters can be approached without too much self-consciousness today as the magical rays of the Moon mingle with those of Mercury. Deep disclosures and ardent avowals are expressed with ease, adding to a more complete understanding of someone close. Open your heart and your mind and the affection you receive will make it all worthwhile. Away from more personal intimacies, financial affairs should benefit from a frank talk about investments, insurance policies and bank accounts.

TUESDAY, 26th. An optimistic astral agenda holds out special memories and excited expectations for many, and your Tuesday stars are certainly magical! Nectarine Neptune is in on the astral act and all Leos will want to take things very easy in order to give divine daydreams and inspired imagination a chance. There could be a powerful passion bubbling deliciously beneath the surface, too!

WEDNESDAY, 27th. If your family fortunes have faltered, check over the facts and figures with an expert adviser and you'll uncover a legal loophole, economic oversight or tangled tax situation that's at the root of the problem. Take ruthless action to set any shared finances on a more sound and stable footing Wednesday and you'll do yourself and others a fiscal favour. An intimate encounter could make your hair curl in the most delightful way!

THURSDAY, 28th. You've begun to realise that the sky's the limit concerning a collaborative effort designed to improve your life all round, but you must also remember that Rome wasn't built in a day! Gigantic Jupiter's stately progress through the heavens is reversed for a few months, putting a few beneficial brakes on your ambitions and allowing you time to attend to the foundations of your plans before they all becomes top heavy and too airy fairy. Travel plans may have to be shelved or postponed if they are eventually to succeed.

FRIDAY, 29th. A casual chat with your other half about the state of the world in general will put you on the trail of a few practical and positive steps you can take to do your bit in your own life, whether it's cutting out pesticides in your garden, joining a pressure group or resolving to become better informed on current affairs. It may seem a small step but it all makes a difference.

SATURDAY, 30th. Mighty Mars emits a burst of avid energy and ignites an outburst of aggressive power from a supercharged Sun. You'll thrill to the rush of adrenaline as you realise that you're in for a battle royal and a show of strength and stamina as a competitive companion issues an irresistible challenge. You'll enjoy a rough and tumble, but don't get carried away. Sometimes you don't know your own strength, Leo!

SUNDAY, 31st. Take it easy! You're as jumpy as a cat on a hot tin roof as your emotions are all fired up and fizzling with activity and agitation! You won't take kindly to any sensible advice or attempts to keep you under control, so I should steer well clear of any china shops if I were you! Future plans on a grand scale are more your scene, so forget about those irritating details just for now and sketch out some grandiose and glorious gambits that will open new doors in your world.

FEBRUARY

MONDAY, 1st. A wee shopping spree is in the stars for you, my friend, as you feel the urge to splash out with your loot and lavish a few luxuries on the one you love. Your cash flow may not run to the most expensive goodies on display, but a cat may look at a king, and a Lion may browse amongst the expensive goodies! In fact, you have terrific taste now and may make a very wise investment, so don't be afraid to let yourself go. You can't put a foot wrong now!

TUESDAY, 2nd. The more cultural and cultivated aspects of life always attract you but you're filled with an added sophistication from Tuesday, thanks to velvet Venus spreading her vernal rays around you. Everything cultural, from music to the visual arts, entrances you over the coming weeks, so try to take in a gallery, theatre or other centre of excellence. Love interests lie abroad.

WEDNESDAY, 3rd. The midweek message offers an abundance of astral encouragement to ensure you and your other half are in close communication about your plans for the future. Chat with anyone close to you about your longterm hopes or meet up with friends who share your deep concerns. If you're dying to meet like-minded pals, why not join a club or society that appeals?

THURSDAY, 4th. Hang out the flags, for Thursday's stars bring a scintillating shower of splendid social successes and opportunities! Open your heart to a loved one and you'll discover a shared path to a golden and glorious future. If you're an independent Lion you shouldn't shun the limelight now, for by being adventurous and audacious you could find yourself a soul mate.

FRIDAY, 5th. A surprise celebration could be sprung on you by your family, who've been hatching this pleasant plot behind your back with the care and precision of a military operation. This is a perfect opportunity to chat with your kinfolk about feelings that are too private and personal to be treated lightly. It'll do them good to get a few things off their chests, whilst you'll be deeply moved when you realise how totally you're trusted.

SATURDAY, 6th. It's showdown time with the partner in your life, whether it's your spouse or a business colleague. The Full Moon in your Sun sign is shining so brightly that you can't ignore anything that isn't working in your relationships any more, and although it can be a bit bothersome, it's a marvellous opportunity to clear the air of any disagreements. Have a heart-to-heart and don't hold back, as you can really get rid of the cobwebs now!

SUNDAY, 7th. A miraculous mental mood ensues as the mastermind Mercury moves into the sign of Pisces this Sunday. Your attention is drawn to fiscal affairs and you can chart a flawless course through a potential minefield of pecuniary problems. Any dealings with big businesses, investment or insurance companies now should turn a profit in your favour. You're such a monetary whizz kid for the next couple of weeks, Leo!

MONDAY, 8th. The Full Moon in your Sun sign opens the doorways to a renewed understanding in all your partnerships, so whether this is a one-to-one intimate affair or a more professional link, it's a case of great minds thinking alike! It is your direction, though, that is important now. If you take decisive action, your firm determination can relieve the anxieties and insecurities of those close. Everybody's happy for you to take the load on your shoulders for a while. You, too, are in your element, organising everything from complex business agenda to an intimate twosome at a favourite nightspot.

TUESDAY, 9th. Your other half will bring you down to earth with a bump as they point out the many chores and purely practical tasks that have been piling up whilst you've been enjoying yourself. There's no avoiding the need to get a few dull but necessary jobs done, so knuckle down to it. It's a splendid opportunity to talk over your long-term ambitions as a couple, for together you make a formidable team. If you're solitary, someone you meet now could seem stern and strict, but don't judge them on first impressions. Never judge a book – or person – by the cover.

WEDNESDAY, 10th. The heavenly green light is egging you on from your house of comings and goings, ensuring a most eventful and effervescent day. Kindly old Jupiter is in league with the sympathetic Moon, stimulating your most sincere and sagacious thoughts. It's a fine day to keep in touch with close relatives or near neighbours, even if it's just to remind them that you care. You could be surprised at how much mutual assistance and home-grown wisdom is available when you take the trouble to ask for it.

THURSDAY, 11th. What a marvellous day simply to stroll around your own neighbourhood, chatting to the friendly folk you meet and passing the time of day with a neighbour. Don't expect to achieve anything too dramatic or drastic with your conversational and chatty approach, but you could pick up a few sensational snippets that'll make you the centre of attention when you talk it all over with your other half.

FRIDAY, 12th. What a kind and considerate bunch your workmates are! Even if you're not amongst the ranks of the employed, the folk you meet with on an everyday basis prove positively pleasant, harmonious and helpful as they go about their daily business. An especially enchanting workmate may tickle your fancy so much you invite them out for a spot of wining and dining, and who knows where it may lead? Ooh la la!

SATURDAY, 13th. Are you happy with the way your domestic life is running? Do you gnash your teeth at the mess in the kitchen or way you always seem to run out of soap? Now's the time to set your domestic world in order and take a long hard look at anything that isn't working around the home, as the stars decree a day of domestic discussion.

SUNDAY, 14th. It may be Valentine's Day but the starry schedule will need a helping hand to get it back on to a romantic course. If you don't take some pretty drastic steps to defuse a tense domestic situation you could find the warpaint coming out as your other half falls foul of fixed family traditions. Perhaps your partner's not quite what was expected or maybe your clan's traditions strike your chosen one as barbaric? Either way, you're the piggy (or should I say Lion?) in the middle, trying to maintain the peace. Above all, avoid taking sides, for this can be sorted out only through care and compromise.

MONDAY, 15th. Your partner in life might not be playing ball about some far-reaching domestic changes that you've been toying with. It's too easy now for a minor difference of opinion to be blown out of all proportion just because you're in one of your stubborn moods. If you were truthful, you would admit that you can be far too determined to get your own way. If you do try to look at it from another angle, you could find that your nearest and dearest's objections have got something in them after all. Try to give a little. Be magnanimous, Leo, you can be so good at that!

TUESDAY, 16th. A quiet word with a child who's been emotionally overwrought will soon smooth over a sensitive situation, for your forthright manner is tempered with tremendous tact today. A little time spent with your other half will be just what's required to confirm that all's well with your world, as harmony prevails in all close personal partnerships now.

WEDNESDAY, 17th. As an organiser of domestic and financial arrangements you're a wise old owl, and can happily help yourself and your family along the road to a stable, secure and happy future now. Business and commercial activities are favoured and if you take the trouble to give luck a helping hand, you could find that the most grandiose and ambitious of your plans are in the realms of possibility.

THURSDAY, 18th. Profound and powerful rays erupt around your solar house of physical relationships and your joint financial areas, too! If you're wanting to sort out these very personal and private areas of your world, do so now. It's a perfect period for deep and involved discussions as well as for sharing your deeper feelings and passions.

FRIDAY, 19th. Listen to any ideas your other half may have that are designed to increase the level of luxury in your lives and produce a more appealing parade of pleasures, for they know what you like and are intent on bringing a smile of sheer happiness to your eyes and lips. It may be a pleasant lunch of all your favourite dishes or a drive in the country, followed by a magnificent meal at a posh restaurant of your choice but, either way, you can count on enjoying yourself!

SATURDAY, 20th. A pouting and peevish partner could be confronting you with an ultimatum or two if you don't set some time aside to lavish your luscious Leonine charm on them. Make sure you find out exactly what's bothering them, even if it takes some patient probing, as some deep emotions will be involved and you need to bring them out into the open to offer the right reassurance. An intense and emotional day.

SUNDAY, 21st. If you've buried or hidden any feelings of emotional or sexual inadequacy, now's the time to sort out such intimate and personal problems before they ruin close personal relationships. You're walking through a minefield of sensitivity now, so tread very warily, as one false move will provoke an explosion that could do enormous damage and set you back years.

MONDAY, 22nd. You're tempted to gain an unfair advantage over someone in authority by using your magnetic charm and compelling charisma, and why not? Anything from planning to take an apple for teacher to fluttering your eyelashes when you bump into your boss will work like a dream and put you firmly into a position of favour. Appeal to the soft and sentimental side of people in power now and you'll advance your aims!

TUESDAY, 23rd. Behind that frank and forthright facade you actually have a very shrewd brain ticking away, so put it to work now solving any problems in your profession. Exploit any contacts you have with folk behind the scenes, as all it takes is a little intelligent inducement to have them pulling strings on your behalf.

WEDNESDAY, 24th. As you go about your business and meet with various people from your own neighbourhood as well as from far afield, you'll become more and more aware of a vague irritation with their conversational customs and outlook on life. It could take a while for you to figure out what's rubbing you up the wrong way and meanwhile you're apt to be a mite snappy, sarcastic and satirical. Try to be more tolerant, for the chances are you're only annoyed by the fact that they're different from you.

THURSDAY, 25th. You can be such a conservative soul at times and you could be missing out on some interesting and useful ideas if you stick solely to the old ways of doing things. Why not make this Thursday a cosmopolitan affair, whether it's by inviting a far-flung relative to your abode or trying a few exotic dishes on your other half.

FRIDAY, 26th. Family affairs and domestic issues are in desperate straits as Pluto ponderously changes course and petulently stamps his foot. Irritating and unreasonable attitudes from some family members will make you see red but losing your rag is definitely the wrong thing to do. You'll only be playing into the hands of someone who is demanding attention. It's far wiser to attempt to have a reasonable talk and sort out whatever lies at the root of this tribal tiff.

SATURDAY, 27th. You've been getting on so well with everyone from your bank manager or your accountant to the love of your life lately but Saturday's wavering wayfarer, wee Mercury, throws a spanner into the works. Every time you try to get a pertinent point across you seem to hit an obstacle and find yourself nattering on about completely irrelevant issues. It's not easy to concentrate whilst you're so distracted, so make allowances for the muddled state of your mind.

SUNDAY, 28th. Some very firm family feelings are activated by Sunday's moody stars and if you're not careful, you'll trigger a tantrum that'll destroy the amiable atmosphere of your home. You're inclined to be inflexible, intransigent and obstinate yourself if your career becomes the topic of conversation, so before you end up at loggerheads with your concerned kinfolk, try some straight talking.

MARCH

MONDAY, 1st. Unexpected visitors may mean well by taking the opportunity to drop in but they're not exactly welcome if you were planning a peaceful time curled up on the sofa or immersed in a good book. You can't turn folk away just because you're feeling reserved and retiring but, with a little tact and diplomacy, you could steer them into leaving a bit early. Take it easy today, for you need to recharge your batteries.

TUESDAY, 2nd. A friend you've always trusted implicitly in the past could strike a false note in something they say or do Tuesday, setting you thinking along suspicious and sceptical lines. Investigate the facts behind some information they give you before you jump to an uncharitable conclusion, for you may not know the whole picture just yet and it wouldn't hurt to give them the benefit of the doubt.

WEDNESDAY, 3rd. Forge forward with any delicate financial negotiations or sensitive situations that are beginning to stagnate. You have the strength now to cut through confusion without treading on too many tender toes. The fervent flames of pure passion are fanned into fiery life by Wednesday's stars, so accept any invitation that could lead to sensual satisfaction and erotic ecstasy.

THURSDAY, 4th. There are some extremely piercing and poignant emotions flowing beneath the surface of your world this Thursday. It almost seems you've a sixth sense of psychic instincts as you tune into the true meaning of a loved one's casual comments or divine the real intentions of a furtive family member. Don't hesitate to mention your insights, if only to see if you're on the right lines. Everyone will be deeply touched that you've seen through the mask to the heart of gold.

FRIDAY, 5th. Luscious lunar rays bathe you in a resplendent radiance as the Moon glides through your own Sun sign. You can temper your natural fiery magnificence now with a gentle and sympathetic charm that will have folk flocking to your side to share in such a divine glow. Family affairs are close to your heart now and you'll instinctively want to do all you can for your kith and kin.

SATURDAY, 6th. While your nearest and dearest are busy putting forward their own point of view over a domestic dispute, you'll be just as firmly fixed on your own position, and if you carry on like that it'll be a case of ne'er the twain shall meet! Make an effort to see things from the standpoint of others and you'll contribute to a delicious détente!

SUNDAY, 7th. Logic has its limitations, as you will easily understand now. You're intuitively aware of all the hidden shades of meaning and irrational emotion lurking lovingly beneath every casual comment, or even a meaningful glance from someone close. They'll be deeply touched that you comprehend the hidden heart of the matter and may well choose to confide certain sensitive secrets. You find it all so fascinating now!

MONDAY, 8th. An intense emotional experience is heralded by the Full Moon bringing to the surface many complexes and psychological blocks from deep inside. It may concern a physical relationship or a professional matter involving joint finances but, wherever your emotions are focused, you have the opportunity to come to terms with your deepest and darkest feelings. It's a mighty sensitive time, when there's much more going on than meets the eye in most situations.

TUESDAY, 9th. If you're normally too busy being your impatient Leonine self to wonder too deeply about what makes you tick, perhaps you should take the opportunity of today's thoughtful and introspective stars to do a little serious thinking. You can understand the hidden motivations behind your actions so much more easily now that everything is becoming much clearer. If you've been putting off some business or financial discussions, this is an excellent time to set the ball rolling and clear up any misunderstandings.

WEDNESDAY, 10th. If you've been having trouble understanding what your other half has been feeling lately, now's your chance to talk things over and find out what the problem is. You're a wee bit confused over your direction in life and a good honest heart-to-heart will help you to clear a path through your doubts and anxieties. Communicate while you've got the chance and you'll lift a weight from your poor burdened shoulders.

THURSDAY, 11th. Voluptuous Venus comes to a celestial standstill and casts a shadow of doubt over the constant flow of pleasure in your life. If you're wondering why folk aren't showering you with affection as much as you'd like this Thursday, the answer lies in this starry stoppage. But don't worry, you'll soon be in the pink again! Patience is rewarded now.

FRIDAY, 12th. As Friday's fervent sky is filled with the intense emotions generated by the pairing of the Moon and Pluto, so you're enveloped in a plethora of powerful, potent and passionate feelings. A nostalgic and sentimental comment uttered by a family member, a memento from the past or perhaps a photo album all conspire to show you how deeply your heritage has affected you. It warms the cockles of your heart to know how firmly your family background is rooted in a glorious and golden past!

SATURDAY, 13th. A colleague or friend will be bubbling with the brightest of brainwaves now, inspiring you to see all sorts of new ways to adjust your economic strategy to advantage. This is no time to stick to the tried and trusted ways of accounting – a novel approach will help you see the problems in a whole new and appealing light. Experiment and investigate!

SUNDAY, 14th. Instigate a searching scrutiny of your subconscious state, for you may uncover a long-buried belief or assumption that's been leading you astray. Turn your astute and observant mind to mastering shared monetary matters and you'll soon convert trouble and strife to cash acquiescence as you come to terms with the root causes of conflict. You're so money-minded and fiscally astute today.

MONDAY, 15th. Your nerves may not be frayed and frazzled today but even so, you're still not back to your usual placid and peaceable self. What you really need is a quiet Monday spent far from the hustle and bustle of the world, but some folk seem incapable of leaving you to your own devices. It may not always be easy to keep a civil tongue in your head, but you won't get anywhere by getting all hot and bothered.

TUESDAY, 16th. As you and your family gradually grow and mature there are certain adjustments to be made in the way you all treat each other, and Tuesday's stars bring an excellent chance for you all to face up to this fact. It's so easy not to adapt to changing emotional and economic circumstances affecting you and your kith and kin, but don't evade the issue.

WEDNESDAY, 17th. Today's starry aspects are splendid for getting many grey areas of your life sparkling with a more colourful glow. For instance, your working world should be tackled with a forthrightness that will give it an injection of efficiency, precision and organisation. From having a good tidy-up to getting on with your fellow workers, help turn over a new leaf in your job.

THURSDAY, 18th. Like a celestial seesaw the planets produce a totally different day, inundated with optimism and brimming over with beaming good humour! You could be so relieved to find an opening in the obstacles surrounding you that you'll leap at the chance to alleviate your problems without thinking things through. You'll land in some mighty hot water if you take too much on trust, so take a canny, cautious and careful attitude to any opportunity now.

FRIDAY, 19th. You're an affable and ardent Lion under these sociable stars as the Moon's tender rays are happily boosted by jocular Jupiter. If you haven't got a party or shindig planned, make sure you get out and socialise, as you're a real sparkling charmer today. A loved one brings a beneficial bonus to brighten the day's news.

SATURDAY, 20th. The symbolism of those golden daffodils dancing in the springtime breeze seems to say to you that now's the time to get out of your restricting ruts, break away from the bonds that bind you, spread your wings and fly! For you this means embarking on a journey, either physical or mental, that will broaden your concepts of the world and life.

SUNDAY, 21st. The Moon meets up with Mercury today and endows you with an exquisite ability to understand any hidden meanings in the words or world of people around you. You're psychic! Equally, your own deep feelings will be revealed to anyone with a modicum of perception, so take care. An incredibly intuitive Sunday invites you to scrutinise submerged sensitivity.

MONDAY, 22nd. Your valiant efforts to understand precisely where you stand with a mysterious lover or potential backers with a fine line of misinformation finally begin to bear comprehensible fruit. The zodiac's mini master of communications is back on the forward track and, as a result, you're finally beginning to make sense of some very complex situations. You have until mid-May to focus your intellectual expertise on such esoterica as shared finances, tax affairs or insurance.

91

TUESDAY, 23rd. Fresh fields and verdant pastures are just over the horizon, as you've reached a point in your life when you must expand your scope or miss the boat. It's time to take up a stimulating study, travel overseas or push back the mental and physical parameters of your present world. Why fret at the frontiers of knowledge when you can look beyond the borders?

WEDNESDAY, 24th. You're positively glowing with optimism and enthusiasm as you're finally convinced that the world really is your oyster! You feel the need to expand your emotional and mental horizons, so get out and about and meet as many people as possible. You can't bear to waste time sitting at home, so go out and circulate or you'll end up with a massive phone bill!

THURSDAY, 25th. Has your partner in life turned green lately? I don't mean literally, but ecological concerns are beginning to worry us all and the stars indicate a supremely sensible ray illuminating your solar house of one-to-one affairs. Normally you're inclined to dismiss their anxieties as too pessimistic but maybe you should get more informed about the issues? Follow the lead of your other half and they'll open your eyes to certain important facts.

FRIDAY, 26th. Your friendly bank manager really is a pillar of society, and Friday you discover you can talk about your financial affairs with ease as they find an understanding and favourable audience. Your plans may be ambitious but, with the right advice, they could be very lucrative, so make sure you listen as well as talk to potential advisers.

SATURDAY, 27th. Professional pressures begin to build up and the harder you try to make the grade the more you seem to be pushing up against a solid brick wall. Rely on support from your colleagues and you'll be able to smooth the path forwards, though you'll have to overcome resistance from a partner first. Concentrate on career moves and you'll at least find out what it is that you're up against.

SUNDAY, 28th. Surround yourself with an admiring audience of faithful friends Sunday and you'll reach the heights of happiness, as popularity's your birthright and you naturally expect to take centre stage in any social gathering. You need to feel that you belong to a wider family than your own personal clan so, if your crowd of chums seems a mite meagre, why not join a club or society that'll widen your social horizons?

MONDAY, 29th. Future hopes and wishes get you all fired up with enthusiasm only to meet with a bucket of cold water when you try to work things out logically and practically. Your head is intent on working things out in a sensible and well-organised way while your heart is leaping ahead, eager to explore. Try to strike a happy medium and you will go far!

TUESDAY, 30th. Get out and about in search of a little common sense and straight talking Tuesday and you'll encounter an old friend whose words of wisdom are just what you need to put you in the picture. Once you realise how many folk there are with their heads screwed on properly you'll be tempted to join in a group or club devoted to some positive practical pursuits. Teamwork's terrific now!

WEDNESDAY, 31st. Past passions and long-forgotten feelings lie in wait this weekend, waiting to trip you up as you try get on with the thousand and one little jobs involved in your day-to-day round. Don't neglect your inner equanimity, as subconscious worries could have a way of making their perplexing presence felt just when you're not expecting it. A sensitive day, so take some time for reflection and calm contemplation.

APRIL

THURSDAY, 1st. A faraway look comes into your eyes Thursday as voluptuous Venusian vibes veer your thoughts into an escapist dream. If you can manage an early spring break, away from the toil and trouble of everyday chores, you'll be in your element, for pleasure now lies chiefly in exploration and adventure. Escape into the wonderful world of your imagination if you can't jet off to the sun, for you're inspried with many beautiful ideas and images. Nothing should be carried too far, though. We don't want you turning into an April fool, do we?

FRIDAY, 2nd. A friend's unusual attitude will be very puzzling today, and he or she may be withdrawn or snappy. Don't worry, it's nothing to do with you or anything that you've done. It's just that there are some delicate personal affairs lurking in the background of their lives. It's hard to approach such a ticklish topic, so hold yourself back and wait. It's important to be there if your friend wants a shoulder to cry on or just needs to talk. Remember that a friend in need is a friend indeed, and you can be such a precious pal!

SATURDAY, 3rd. Be careful today as it seems someone in authority is gunning for you. There is a certain coolness in the air, so don't think that you can get away with anything, as a rather humourless person seems to have it in for you. Stay away from any scenes of trouble or where you may flare up with a display of dramatic Leonine passion. My, you can roar so loudly!

SUNDAY, 4th. It's a laugh a minute as a light-hearted Moon is whisked off her delicate feet by a restless Venus, giving your bubbly personality a delicious boost that will surely set your own feet tapping! Get out and about and enjoy yourself, whether your taste runs to a day at the races or a night at the opera. It's time to have some serious fun!

MONDAY, 5th. The thrilling theme of superb celebration continues right through into Monday. These last few days have given you a golden opportunity to get back in touch with your family or, if they're far away, you've been able to immerse yourself in many precious memories. It all helps to bring long-forgotten incidents to the surface, so share your insights and emotions with the folk who mean so much to you. They'll be deeply touched.

TUESDAY, 6th. Today's Full Moon augurs a shake-up in your world of mammoth mental proportions, as you're obliged to acknowledge any faults, failings or flaws in your outlook on life. Cast out pointless opinions and pursue only that which is positive! This is also the beginning of a sizzling and sexy span as voluptuous Venus imbues your love life with sensual desire.

WEDNESDAY, 7th. It's a chatty, chirpy day when your mind is full of bright ideas and interesting inspirations. You should follow your hunches through now, as you're a skilful sleuth and can find practical uses and sensible solutions for the most unrealistic of ideas and intuitions. Put on your thinking cap and you'll come up with answers to the stickiest problems.

THURSDAY, 8th. A torrent of sweet sentiment rushes you off your feet and engulfs you in a marvellous miasma of nostalgia and poignant melancholy. Take a trip down memory lane and wallow in the wonderful emotions from times gone by that your recollections evoke, as it's the past that holds you in its spell now. You'll feel all the better for a renewed acquaintance with your past glories.

FRIDAY, 9th. A family skeleton in the closet is the subject of secret negotiations that could do you nothing but good, bringing you closer to your kith and kin. Legal eagles are doing marvellous work behind the scenes on your behalf, but make sure your partner doesn't feel too mystified and left out of it all, as in their present negative frame of mind he or she will probably assume the worst.

SATURDAY, 10th. Get the glad rags out, for the luscious lunar light illuminates the allure of lovely Venus. You can expect an invitation popped in the post, so put on your brightest smile and prepare to party. You will be sought after by many now, and if you aren't invited to the very best gatherings, then I'm not the stargazer you take me for! You have an instructive ability to be at your charming best, and if you have any artistic or poetic leanings, this is the day to give them full rein. You're such a popular Lion now.

SUNDAY, 11th. Whilst most folk are taking things very easy today after all the fantastic fun and frolics, you're proving what a sensible Lion you are by getting on with a few important tasks and helpful errands. If you've a partner in life or spouse close by, make a point of showing them this superb streak of common sense. They'll be very impressed with your orderly and pragmatic outlook.

MONDAY, 12th. Such a conniving sky as today's couldn't possibly be relied upon for anything concrete or matter of fact. You must be careful of giving the wrong impression, as although it is quite likely you could be taken in by others, you could equally be playing spurious games without knowing it. It's not as straightforward as you would like it today, but you must admit that you can be such a wicked soul yourself!

TUESDAY, 13th. There is an urge within you, making you crave to get away and do something different. Judging by the starry pattern above you, nobody could persuade you to be cool, calm and collected today. Be warned that your own nervous disposition may make you bring extra stress upon yourself out of desperation. Even if you can't face the trials of the world in a reasonable and rational fashion, it's important that you try. A few deep breaths at the appropriate moment will work wonders to relieve your levels of stress.

WEDNESDAY, 14th. It's a Wednesday for getting deep-rooted feelings out into the open, so don't play your cards close to your chest or refuse to accept your emotions. Thrash out any sexual or intimate problems with your partner while you can put your inmost feelings into words. Subjects that otherwise would be a source of embarrassment can be discussed in a calm, matter-of-fact fashion now. Mystical, supernatural or spiritual subjects fascinate you now as you're drawn to anything mysterious. Sometimes it's the weirder the better for you!

THURSDAY, 15th. Masterful young Mercury marches boldly into your horoscope's house of travel and exploration, bringing a period when you're mentally stimulated to stretch the frontiers of your world in all areas. This is a splendid time for journeys, especially if you're contemplating a long-distance trek. Also, you could be receiving news from afar that leads to a celebration.

FRIDAY, 16th. The only cloud on your horizon at the moment is the vexed question of your close personal partnerships for, though you try to make a positive impression and introduce a mood of optimism, it seems you're beating your head against a brick wall. With cautious care and patient persistence you'll be able to lift the aura of gloom and rearrange your relationships in a constructive and rewarding way, so don't let an overly emotional response wreck your chances.

SATURDAY, 17th. You're an instinctive and intuitive genius this Saturday, for you know with unerring accuracy just when openly to promote your incredibly ambitious ideas and when to rely on more subtle methods of manipulation. On the surface, folk will think you're just drifting along but actually you're in total control, feeding folk the ideas and information that will make them play right into your hands. Make sure you use your sensitive skills to benefit others as well as yourself and the world will be your oyster!

SUNDAY, 18th. Leos with passionate partners should set time aside this sizzling Sunday for an erotic interlude, for your red-hot nature's primed by the sensational stars. If that's not your cup of tea, direct your intense energies into a fascinating mystery or intriguing investigation. Anything from a cunning detective novel to the intricacies of your tax affairs will make a fitting challenge for your sleuthing skills now.

MONDAY, 19th. Your personal integrity is always important to you but never more so than now, when you can clearly understand how much your emotional security depends on being in the right. Don't be content with outdated ideas of right and wrong, though, as this is a domain of doctrine that's ready to be explored much more thoroughly, and you're the wise Lion for the task.

TUESDAY, 20th. An upsurge in your already astounding ambitions comes about today as the sunny rays of your own personal starry ruler enter your horoscopic house of career. If you haven't been too satisfied with the direction of your professional life, now's the time to think of making some far-reaching changes. Lions who are presently unemployed will find the next few weeks a much more promising period for your prospects. Whatever your circumstances, the lure of a new vocation promising greater achievement will provide a strong appeal.

WEDNESDAY, 21st. The celestial emphasis today is very much on your business affairs as the New Moon brings a forceful focus of energies to help you make a fresh beginning of some sort. It's a wonderful day to lay the groundwork or foundations for your future plans, so see what you can do to have a word with the boss, or perhaps take the first steps in some entirely new business venture. It's a time to start a fresh career cycle, even though your ego's extra-sensitive, so seek a new direction and prepare to be amazed with the ease of your achievements.

THURSDAY, 22nd. The goddess of amour, velvet Venus, steers a more direct course from today and smooths the way for love in your life. Why seek a soul mate close to home? You could find there are so many potential sweethearts out in the wide world that the charms of the girl (or boy) next door pale rapidly into insignificance. Be a little more adventurous where romance is concerned and ravishing rapture can rapidly be yours!

FRIDAY, 23rd. You feel a need to have your efforts recognised and to be praised and rewarded by folk you admire and respect. A figure of paternal authority or perhaps your own father plays a large part in your life Friday, and you yearn to show him you're capable of living up to the faith he has in you. Career and business matters are tailored to boost your ego.

SATURDAY, 24th. Your sense of drama will come in very handy today as you are pushed into the spotlight. Or should I say you push yourself, because you're never at the back of the queue when it comes to putting your best foot forward! Be that as it may, you'll be fired with enthusiasm and well prepared to act as a sort of spokesperson for others of a shyer diposition. You can give this one your all. If it was up to me, I'd put you up for at least an Oscar nomination!

SUNDAY, 25th. In contrast to yesterday's uplifting astral influence, today's starry schedule brings you into contact with a friend who seems to think that you are a walking bank balance. Never a borrower or a lender be, is my advice for you Sunday. If you think you're being taken for a ride, the time has come to point out a few of the more unpalatable facts of life to someone who seems to think that money, especially yours, grows on trees.

MONDAY, 26th. Professional pressures are cutting you off from the folk you hold near and dear, forcing you to choose between them and your career plans. You feel lonely and weary and ready to give up but, if you just hang on a bit longer, you'll see that most of your fears are all in the mind. Don't magnify your problems – you'll be more than ready to meet the challenge when you're feeling stronger.

TUESDAY, 27th. Assertive Mars speeds his way into your Sun sign, which is excellent news for all personal projects and aspir-ations. You should take the initiative now, as you want to get on with the job in question. Sudden decisions and actions are much better than doing nowt. If you make a mistake in your onward rush, don't fret, as all can be put right later. Right now, actions speak louder than words and it's vital that you aren't thought of as a ditherer.

WEDNESDAY, 28th. Superficially at least, your world is totally tranquil and serene today. As in anyone's life, there are hidden depths and sensitive secrets affecting family relations and domestic details, but that's no cause for conflict. Use your inside information on a relative's situation to proffer a little moral support. A word of understanding will go a long way to relieving worries and tensions, so be a magnanimous Lion. You're so good at that!

THURSDAY, 29th. Are you tired of the rat race, weary of the struggle to make your mark on an uncaring and indifferent world? It's a good thing it's almost the weekend, for you'll find all you really need is some rest and recreation to restore your emotional equilibrium. You're inclined to be oversensitive about the opinions others hold of you now, so try not to take it all too much to heart.

FRIDAY, 30th. Today's merry mood could be dampened for good by your wet blanket of a partner if you take their carping criticisms and disparaging disapproval too much to heart. They don't necessarily mean to bring you down to earth with such a leaden thud but they can't help pondering the practical problems involved in a long-term plan you're evolving. Give them a chance to air their anxieties and they'll feel so much better, and then you can get on with it!

MAY

SATURDAY, 1st. So begins the merry month of May and a few moments spent updating your chequebook or putting your purse in order will bring you peace of mind now, as you quickly feel uneasy and insecure when you sense that your money's in disarray. You need to know precisely where you stand financially, as any uncertainty weighs you down with worry, so take the opportunity of a contemplative day to attend to your finances.

SUNDAY, 2nd. If your wallet's as thin as a rake and all your accounts empty and echoing, call on the economic aid of your family. They may give you a straightforward injection of cash to help you through a temporary time of pecuniary privation. Failing this, a well-meaning relative could help you sort out the underlying cause of your financial failings and assist you to devise a more productive budgetary approach.

MONDAY, 3rd. The harbinger of communications bustles into your house of career and ambition, handing you a businesslike period when you can get your ideas across in an impressive and constructive way. Whatever your aspirations, you're mentally astute and shrewd enough to talk your way into the position you seek. Arrange business meetings or interviews and you'll meet with the approval of those who matter.

TUESDAY, 4th. Your life should be on a very agreeably even keel this Tuesday as you get on with your everyday tasks and enjoy the satisfaction of knowing you're fulfilling your obligations and responsibilities. You may even make a few gains in a professional aim as you impress a superior with your well-balanced and supremely sensible attitude.

WEDNESDAY, 5th. Your feelings are as real and important to you as the most solid piece of furniture in your home, but it's not always easy for you to let others know just what emotions are enveloping you, since you would so hate to be misunderstood or mocked. Your partner in life can show what an understanding soul he or she is now as you feel you can unburden some of your anxieties without taking too much of a risk. Solitary Lions should seek a pal who can lend an ear.

THURSDAY, 6th. Grasp the bull by the horns today and seize the chance to discuss any domestic, emotional or practical problems that hold your clan back as a whole. Only by eliminating outworn attitudes to each other will you present a united front to the world.

Speak with someone in authority about a high-powered pecuniary and professional plan you're developing and they'll be very impressed with your insight, not to mention your audacity.

FRIDAY, 7th. Anyone would think you were stuck in the Ice Ages as you frown and fret with the weight of the world on your shoulders. You need to sort out a few practical problems pertaining to your personal partnerships, but that's no reason to go around with such a long face. Cheer up – a positive outlook is half the battle when it comes to overcoming obstacles of any kind.

SATURDAY, 8th. A love of the arts, music and easy-going people is highlighted Saturday, making you realise that enjoyment is an important part of life. Time spent playing with children or helping them with a pet project will bring you closer together. Don't neglect your own personal hobbies, for you have a creative itch that needs to be scratched. Love affairs flourish under such sensitive and sensual skies.

SUNDAY, 9th. Spread your personal net of contacts far and wide, for Sunday's stars herald a day of divine opportunity and positively constructive communications. Tune in to the thoughts of anyone you encounter now and you'll hear news and views that are very much to your advantage. Motivate your neighbours in developing local amenities, for united action wins the day.

MONDAY, 10th. Yesterday's encouraging trends continue, helping you to consolidate your gains and widen your circle of contacts. This is a splendid opportunity to think about overseas travel plans, as you're in an adventurous mood and won't let too many petty considerations about time and money stand in the way of your enterprising urge. Maybe an out-of-season holiday would fit the bill?

TUESDAY, 11th. Emotionally you'll be on tenterhooks for a wee while as the mystical maiden, the Moon, receives a buffeting at the hands of both Saturn and Uranus. An unsettled and insecure rest-lessness rocks the boat in the morning, but later on you'll be able to talk things through in a much more sensible way. Avoid overreacting to a situation that isn't nearly as gloomy as it seems. It's vital you keep your feet on the ground, so you don't lose your head when all around you seem set on losing theirs over a minor crisis that everyone thinks is a major disaster.

WEDNESDAY, 12th. Full of good intentions to put your best foot forward, this Wednesday you'll be champing at the bit and raring to go. That's all very well until you remember that the rest of us are still a trifle shell-shocked from the emotional upsets of yesterday and would, on the whole, prefer a less energetic introduction to the midweek's bountiful opportunities. Try not to trample on too many tender toes and fragile folk in your rush to reach the top!

THURSDAY, 13th. There's really no way that you can expect things to plod along in the same old way under such excitable and inno-vative stars. Experimental Uranus is given the celestial go-ahead by the majestic Sun and you'll find your world flooded with daring and different ideas to tempt you well away from the beaten track. Don't cling to the familiar now – the path leads forward and holds golden promise for the future.

FRIDAY, 14th. You just can't keep up such a sweeping programme of change and reform in your personal world forever, and today you'll be suffering an emotional backlash as you suddenly feel stuck out on a limb, swaying about in the wind with no sense of security. It's not a position you'd wish on your worst enemy but it's not really as bad as you think, so don't allow a momentary obstacle or setback to invalidate all the progress you've made so far. Things may look black, but could it have something to do with your own well-concealed sense of insecurity?

SATURDAY, 15th. Take a ruthless look at all aspects of your personal and professional life this Saturday and eliminate anything that no longer fits into your scheme of things. That sounds a bit drastic but it's how you'll feel. Maybe you should modify your more merciless impulses with a little more sympathy, for you don't want to end up with a reputation as a power-mad despot!

SUNDAY, 16th. It may be Sunday, the day of rest, but you can't slacken your pace yet, as there's such a fertile flow of fabulously inventive ideas and inspirations to be followed up. Self-employed or solitary Lions should invite a second opinion and discuss the details of plans with others, as two heads are definitely better than one. Healthwise you'll come across a novel new approach that promises much and may even deliver!

MONDAY, 17th. Your irresistible qualities of courage and audacity are at their best now as you're ready to confront any challenge the world throws at you. You excel now at any activity requiring stamina, studying a strenuous subject or projecting your personality. Make sure you've plenty of tough and taxing tasks lined up, as there's no sense in wasting your talents on petty or penny-pinching projects.

TUESDAY, 18th. You can sometimes be a bit of a spoilsport, as you don't like losing and always want to be up there on the winner's rostrum! From Tuesday on you'll have plenty of chances to interact with friends and folk in clubs, where you'll be asked to demonstrate your organisational prowess and display the championship form that you pride yourself on. The more sociable you are now the better.

WEDNESDAY, 19th. As your other half reminds you once again about the details of a projected journey, don't dismiss them as being needlessly timid and timorous, for in fact they know what you're like when the light of adventure fills your eye! Take their advice and make extra sure that everything, from the tickets to an extra pair of socks, is all properly packed and accounted for. People in your world are a rock of security to help you make the most of your opportunities now.

THURSDAY, 20th. I know you won't get anywhere in this world without treading on a few toes, but your brash and bold bearing could irritate some staid establishment folk if you're not careful. By all means show them that you mean business but, at the same time, you must demonstrate a touch more tact if you're to achieve the success you feel you deserve. Steady as you go, Leo!

FRIDAY, 21st. Sunny rays sparkle splendidly into your solar house of the future, giving you the dynamism to tackle plans and projects that could determine where you go from here. Over the next few weeks you must deal exclusively with matters that could make you a very rich and famous pussycat if promoted and projected in the right way. Look to the future, Leo!

SATURDAY, 22nd. Unfinished business or overlooked flaws fall into focus financially and, if you're wise, you'll seize the chance to iron out any wrinkles in tax, investment or inheritance matters. Intimate affairs are under a sober celestial shadow and could place some heavy burdens on your shoulders. You must learn to stand on your own two feet over the next few months.

SUNDAY, 23rd. You and your other half have come to a stalemate regarding your shared ambitions and professional plans, and the only way out of a deadlocked situation is through serious and far-reaching discussion. There's no point living in hope that ignoring your differences will make them go away, as they just won't. Set plenty of time aside to talk over your personal professional aims and bring them into line with your partnership policy.

MONDAY, 24th. I know you've achieved miracles lately with your wonderful wit and intelligent insight, but are you sure your hat size hasn't grown a few inches in the process? Don't let recent successes go to your head now or you may find you've bitten off far more than you can chew. Someone who's out to play on your sympathies should be kept at arm's length, for your resistance to emotional blackmail is nil now!

TUESDAY, 25th. A vivid dream could leave a lasting impression, helping you to comprehend many a mystery buried in your past. Or maybe you flick through some old snapshots and stir up some poignant and moving memories? This is a divine day for delving into your roots in order to understand yourself and your loved ones better.

WEDNESDAY, 26th. Put a red ring round today's date in your diary, for if the sensational stars are anything to go by it's all set to be a red-letter day of tremendous positive potential. It's through being in communication with the people in your life, from a nearby neighbour to penfriends and casual acquaintances, that you'll reap the richest rewards as they stimulate your marvellous mental powers and introduce brand-new ideas that open up a vast vista of possibilities to you. Be confident and self-assured now and terrific triumphs can be yours.

THURSDAY, 27th. Thursday's super-sensitive stars highlight some of the deep-rooted differences between you and your nearest and dearest. It's a little uncomfortable to realise how far you've all come from the early days of unthinking unity and accord, but it's a mistake to hark back continually to past perfections. Nostalgia and sentimentality have no place in your go-ahead world, so try a spot of straight talking with a relative who's too wrapped up in the past to face up to the present.

FRIDAY, 28th. Fun-loving friends have been a bundle of laughs lately but if you're not careful you could be left counting the cost as they leave you to foot the bill. You're reluctant to allow purely pecuniary problems to interfere with the entertainment, but fair's fair and it's high time someone else chipped in with some cash. Your pals will be a lot more understanding than you suppose, so don't be too shy to mention the taboo topic of money!

SATURDAY, 29th. It's boodle all the way now, and you should concentrate on any monetary matters that have eluded you of late.

If you're expecting a cheque or a giro that just hasn't come through, now's the time to get to the bottom of it and sort things out to your satisfaction. However formal it may seem, financial assistance to a friend or colleague should be placed firmly on a businesslike and properly documented basis, rather than letting your heart rule your head.

SUNDAY, 30th. Benevolent generosity oozes from every pore as you understand the power of positive thinking and feel good enough to put it into practice wherever you go. Anyone you bump into will be charmed and delighted and may also have a useful idea or helpful piece of news to speed you on your way. Travel tickles your fancy and offers bounteous benefits.

MONDAY, 31st. You're known as one of the most charismatic and audacious personalities of the zodiac and today we can all see why as your charming tongue appears to be supercharged! You're full to bursting with ideas and thoughts and just can't bear to keep them to yourself. Use your wonderful mental energy creatively and you could be a persuasive and most successful wee Lion as folk bend an ear and are impressed by your enthusiasm.

JUNE

TUESDAY, 1st. Every pace you've made forwards in your life lately has been followed by a wee slippage back, partly due to Jupiter's uncertain progress. All that's a thing of the past from today as Jupiter's gigantic bulk gets back to the benevolent business of boosting your neighbourhood status and mental mastery. This is a fabulous time to look at increasing your educational qualifications or standards. Maybe you could learn a new language to help you on your summer hols? What a cosmopolitan pussycat!

WEDNESDAY, 2nd. Mercury's meandering ways take him into the most secretive and sensitive area of your solar horoscope from today, putting you in the perfect position for finding out what makes you tick. It's not a case of gazing pointlessly at your navel, for by bringing submerged feelings and automatic assumptions into the light of your own consciousness, you can gain a much greater measure of self-control and self-knowledge.

THURSDAY, 3rd. Household harmony dominates the scene as you tune in to all areas of discord and deep resentment among your kith and kin. Everything may seem hunky-dory on the surface, but you know better as your finger is firmly on the pulse of the powerful emotional undercurrents. Don't be drawn into a fight that can't be won – emotional blackmail is rife and you'll all have to be strong to withstand the temptation to get your own way through subtle manipulation.

FRIDAY, 4th. The Full Moon in your horoscopic house of love affairs forces you to face up to a romantic situation that's going nowhere fast and to clear out any emotional rubble and debris that's blocking the free flow of affection. A youngster confronted with a make-or-break decision may need advice and support.

SATURDAY, 5th. There's no two ways about it, you're all set for a smashing Saturday! You're in the mood for enjoying yourself and, by gum, you're determined to do it! Work goes by the board now as you're feeling wonderfully lazy, but don't fall foul of the boss. The only hard work you'll do is when you tuck into grub galore or gallons of grog with someone special.

SUNDAY, 6th. As warm-hearted Venus trots into Taurus today your whole professional world is given a heavenly bonus. Disputes at work or with folk in authority can be soothed and smoothed by the balm of the diplomatic goddess of peace, leaving you with an amiable and affectionate settlement to boost your confidence. Women are especially understanding and helpful in the weeks ahead.

MONDAY, 7th. It could be that a change is due in your domestic world, so instead of puzzling and worrying over what it might mean, sit down and work out in detail just what's needed to transform your home life for the better. A superficial solution isn't the answer, as only a complete move or some major construction work holds the key to your question. It's a very challenging outlook, but you'll find that the rewards are worth the sacrifices!

TUESDAY, 8th. Rather than have your partner worried about an upsurge of jovial sociabilities in your life, why not invite him or her along and put paid to those unfounded suspicions? You're an affectionate wee Lion anyway, and want to do whatever it takes to ensure domestic bliss and romantic rapture. Professional perks give a welcome boost to your finances.

WEDNESDAY, 9th. Superficial chatter is a joy and a delight but beneath the surface some more serious and sinister emotions are stirring. Investigate anything that arouses intense and fanatical feelings in your homely habitat, as something's afoot and it can be resolved only by being brought out into the open. Don't take no for an answer in your quest for the truth.

THURSDAY, 10th. Your steamy sensual stamina could come to an untimely halt now as Saturn turns tail and heads backwards, steaming out of Pisces at a rate of knots. Intimate affairs of all kinds are affected by this unwished-for occurrence. Be they sexual links or private business matters, the retrograde motion of the ringed planet calls many of your well-thought-out plans and intentions into question now. Perhaps you should take this opportunity for a rethink. A review of your position might be helpful in the long run, and save you some costly mistakes.

FRIDAY, 11th. It's a bustling and busy sort of day, in a quiet and sensitive way, as the rays of the Moon combine harmoniously with those of inquisitive Mercury. It's the deeper, more mysterious things in life that hold your interest now as your imagination roams restlessly through the secret and private realms of your subconscious and your innermost feelings. You can express your feelings today with a subtlety and passion that shows your sincerity and proves there's nothing superficial about your innermost emotions.

SATURDAY, 12th. You've put your all into your various activities this past week and, quite honestly, you're beginning to burn the candle at both ends. You can't carry on living in an intense emotional and physical atmosphere without feeling the strain, so take a tip from some of your more laid-back chums and put your feet up this Saturday. There's nothing to be gained from fretting and you can't expect to operate at peak efficiency whilst you're stretched to the limit.

SUNDAY, 13th. It's the principle of the matter that gets you hot under the collar, as you're deeply attached to your beliefs and ideals and want to do all you can to demonstrate your devotion. You need to be given plenty of scope, as you're not at all content to do things in a small and mean way, so volunteer to organise the church bazaar or immerse yourself in profound and worthy literature to satisfy your yearnings.

MONDAY, 14th. It's no simple task to get your message across now as those Mercurial beams run into a damp patch of doubt and denial that'll have you scratching your head. So long as you stick to essentials and make sure that the principle of the matter has been communicated don't worry too much over the details – the chances are they'll look after themselves, anyway.

TUESDAY, 15th. As yesterday's mist lifts you're made aware of a vista of possibilities and potential stretched far out from your feet, tempting you to strike out on a more adventurous path. You won't put a foot wrong if you pursue a policy of exploration, whether it's through religious reform, international inklings or intellectual improvement. Rise to the challenge, Leo!

WEDNESDAY, 16th. With all the doorways of opportunity opening to you now, it's important that you don't just rush in, for you could end up where angels fear to tread. Take your tip from that sober ringmaster Saturn, pause in your onward advance and think deeply about what it is you actually want to achieve. It's true to say that you can't have everything, so it's important that you make the right decisions at the right time. A time to ponder your options deeply, Leo!

THURSDAY, 17th. You're ready to launch yourself at a professional goal to win the prize of success, come what may, but the folk you want to impress are in a sensitive state and are seeking a display of conscience as well as charisma. It's irritating to consider the feelings of others when you're such an eager beaver, but there's no point in antagonising people in power.

FRIDAY, 18th. The Sun and Mars form a potent pair in Friday's sky, injecting an exhilarating air of urgency and excitement into your personal interests and activities. There's a spring in your step and a sparkle in your eye as you pinpoint a challenge and promptly rise to meet it, whether it's leading your friends to a more effective role in pursuing a shared ideal or branching out in a brand-new direction. You're supercharged and sizzling now!

SATURDAY, 19th. You may be fond of your pals but that's no reason to put up with their aimless apathy when you're around to take the lead and instil in them a more ardent, audacious and avid approach. Set an example with your energetic and resolute approach to a personal problem, whether it's physical fitness or your appearance that's causing concern. Socially, you're hot property!

SUNDAY, 20th. A friend in need is a friend indeed, and that's just what you're feeling in need of now! The New Moon in your solar house of group activities may leave you aware of a gap in your life, so do take the opportunity to get out and about so you can meet someone fresh and interesting who could become your best buddy. If ideas concerning personal hopes and wishes for the future have been reduced to a stale, stymied and static state, be prepared to have a reforming think today, as the time is excellent for a review of current concepts and concerns.

MONDAY, 21st. Luscious Lions who are happier away from the turbulent tumult of the world will enjoy life to the full from Monday. Holidays that are taken away from crowded beaches or overflowing tourist traps will be much more enjoyable as you want to retreat from all garish and gaudy destinations. Even if you're a fun-loving pussycat it might be as well to hibernate for a while.

TUESDAY, 22nd. What a super-sensitive wee soul you are this Tuesday! Psychic impulses disturb the surface of your mind and make you wonder just what's real and what's rooted in fantasy. There's no easy answer to that universal riddle but you do have a golden opportunity to reflect on the emotional state of your inner world, as any insights you arrive at now may well be both illuminating and enlightening.

WEDNESDAY, 23rd. The sunny side of your financial street beckons to you now as masterful Mars marches boldly into Virgo, enabling you to leave your worries on the economic doorstep and brighten your pecuniary prospects. If you put all of your vim, vigour and vitality into moneymaking activities, you need never go short again but if for one moment you slip into a reckless, feckless and slapdash fiscal style, you'll undo all your good work.

THURSDAY, 24th. Impulsive, impetuous and extravagant, that's your mood Thursday! Financial limitations will fall instantly by the wayside when your eye lights on an object or treat that's just what you want, for your desires are urgent and insistent and will easily overcome the calm, quiet voice of caution! Don't flare up at anyone who tries to remind you of the economic facts of life – they mean well, even if they do get on your nerves!

FRIDAY, 25th. Peace and harmony reign in the heavens and you're at ease with the world. Finances are giving a warm and rosy glow to your wallet as you find that folk at work are willing to do all they can to help you along. It's a friendly, generous and affectionate day, with the focus on the values you hold dear in life, so whether it's material matters or emotional principles that concern you, you can feel that your world is secure.

SATURDAY, 26th. Now you've thought through certain points, perhaps you're ready to explain your position to other interested parties? It's never easy to speak about spiritual or psychological subjects, but today you've a better chance than usual of conveying some of the salient points in your personal outlook. On a purely practical level, you have second sight when it comes to picking out a bargain!

SUNDAY, 27th. You're not about to broadcast the fact far and wide but you do have a sentimental and sensitive streak, and under Sunday's emotional astral array you're acutely aware of the hidden messages behind people's words. You can tell at a glance what folk really feel, whatever they may say, but if you're wise you'll keep your insights to yourself, for you may only make a delicate situation worse if you speak up.

MONDAY, 28th. Not being afraid to express your view can be a mixed blessing, because today you're likely to let your tongue rattle on a few paces ahead of your mind. Normally this does no harm, but Monday's slightly touchy and tense heavens could lead you into making an embarrassing faux pas by letting slip a secret you've been entrusted with. Do try to put your brain into gear before you open your mouth, however much folk you meet try to goad you into gossip!

TUESDAY, 29th. Events that occur today will convince you that where you work it's really a case of one for all and all for one. There's no future in an entirely egotistical attitude to your everyday activities. Instead, it's by presenting an image of unshakable solidarity with co-workers, customers and clients that you'll all benefit, so throw in your lot with your fellows. It may mean sacrificing immediate and obvious gains for long-term security.

WEDNESDAY, 30th. You may have thought that you'd come to a new understanding in your one-to-one affairs, but Saturn isn't quite through with you yet. He casts a searching glance behind and highlights any false assumptions or rushed resolutions and forces you to go back and do any hasty job properly. Relationships can't continue unless you review your shared rules.

JULY

THURSDAY, 1st. Mentally you're just not at your brilliant best Thursday as mini Mercury goes walkabout in the heavens and casts a cloud of confusion over all attempts at communication. If you've urgent messages and errands that can't wait, take your time and make sure the arrangements are watertight, especially if you're trying to help someone who's inclined to be unreliable.

FRIDAY, 2nd. Hang out the flags and welcome the weekend with open arms, for fun is right at the top of your astral agenda! Pick out your prettiest party frock or most stunning shirt and prepare to be the star of the show, whether it's an informal gathering of cheerful chums or a more elegant outing. If your diary's bare of invites, why not have a few friendly folk round to your place for a wee chat?

SATURDAY, 3rd. Far-reaching changes and useful alterations at work *must* be made if you are to reach the happy heights of job satisfaction and personal fulfilment that seem to be eluding you at present. You cannot go on in the way you have been doing, so take the bull by the horns and prepare to take action professionally. Health practices you know aren't doing you any good must also be curtailed.

SUNDAY, 4th. If there's a jamboree planned, whether it's a wonderful Sunday outing or just a quick drink in your local, better go easy on the hard stuff as you've got a very weak head today. Have one over the eight and you could start going green around the gills, seeing double or getting covered in confusion when you say something embarrassing and rude to a friend, colleague or relative. Stay as sober as a judge!

MONDAY, 5th. On the one hand there's your emotions and intuitions and on the other there's your logical and rational reason, and today you'll be torn between the two, not quite knowing which to believe. It's a distracting and disconcerting day when communications generally seem uncertain and vague, so it's not a favourable time for delicate and important negotiations. Rather than try to figure it out, why not indulge in a little soothing music? Otherwise, a migraine could be the result.

TUESDAY, 6th. Gregarious, genial and generous are the words that immediately spring to mind when gazing at the stars that shine upon you this Tuesday. Actually, the rest of July will see your social life hot up frantically and you'll be so much in demand you'll be wondering which invitations to accept and which ones gracefully to decline. A deliciously delectable time for friends and lovers.

WEDNESDAY, 7th. You're suffering the aftershocks of your bout of restlessness, for you fear the consequences of any changes you made in the heat of the moment. There's no need to go to the other extreme and refuse to change the smallest details of your relationships, for that won't add to your sense of security in the long run. Don't make major decisions whilst you're in such a worried and weary state.

THURSDAY, 8th. We all like to be popular, but aren't you taking your bid to stay in a pal's good books just a little too far? Remember that friendship is something that can't be bought, and a pal who's constantly calling on your generosity to help them out of a fiscal scrape may be taking you for an expensive ride. Keep your charitable impulses within sensible bounds this Thursday or you could live to regret it.

FRIDAY, 9th. Reserved and reticent, that's you this Friday. It's not that you're afraid to open your mouth but, to be honest, you've got better things to do than engage in superficial chitchat. By tuning in to your instinctive insights regarding an investment opportunity or tax tangle, you'll easily find the most fruitful line to take. Intimate affairs will also benefit enormously from a few quiet moments discreetly discussing future plans.

SATURDAY, 10th. A female friend exerts a calming influence, so seize the chance to unwind in the company of someone soothing. The more you relax, the more you'll realise the value of the softer, more sentimental side of life, so be sure to let your friends know just how much you care for them. It's easy now for you to express your affection without feeling awkward or embarrassed, and your pals will be as pleased as punch!

SUNDAY, 11th. At times like this you're your own worst enemy, as you're apt to grab the wrong end of the stick and then cling on to it with terrific tenacity! Own up to the possibility that you may have misunderstood the true intention and meaning of someone's apparently outrageous comments, for it won't get you anywhere simply to stay on your high horse sulking.

MONDAY, 12th. No one needs to talk to you about common sense this Monday, since that would be like teaching your granny to suck eggs! You comprehend the need for method in all your actions and won't take it amiss when a cautious companion points out certain details that could be corrected in your ideas. What a positive, pragmatic and practical pussycat!

TUESDAY, 13th. The old ways and the tested traditions just aren't good enough for you now as the heavens bring massive pressure to bear on the status quo to make sure we don't all fall into a deadening rut. Radical and revolutionary solutions to problems of self-expression and working worries present themselves, but you must take care not to be too ruthless. A sweeping gesture may be satisfying but it could break valuable structures as well as outdated limitations. Change is in the air!

WEDNESDAY, 14th. No matter how many papers lie in wait for you in your in-tray or bulging briefcase, you know that a day's total rest and relaxation is essential to keep you at your efficient and effective best. Put all thoughts of your ambitions to one side and immerse yourself in peace and quiet. You'll perk up visibly as your emotional and physical batteries become recharged.

THURSDAY, 15th. If there's a youngster in the family or in your near neighbourhood, you should hang on their every word Thursday. They seem so much older than their years and can come up with insightful ideas of marvellous maturity and perception. A private chat with someone you've fallen out with will help you heal even deep and festering wounds and improve your level of mutual understanding.

FRIDAY, 16th. It seems to me you've got out of bed on the wrong side this morning, and no amount of kind words and generous gestures is going to sweeten your terrific temper. Brave pals making the valiant attempt will retire with stinging ears and a startled expression as you let fly at just about anyone coming within range. I know you're in a mighty irritable and irascible state, but do they really deserve such rough treatment? Moderate your language or you could put a strain on a close partnership, and then you'd be the loser.

SATURDAY, 17th. Two heads are better than one, Leo – yes, even you could do with a little extra advice and assistance today! There are well-informed acquaintances, professional pals and supremely sensible partners at our beck and call, so use them to the full and ask them for advice. They'll be only too happy to oblige, as they have oodles of experience to draw on and can come up with just the personal and professional pointers you require.

SUNDAY, 18th. A romantic reverie envelops you in a Utopian dream of perfection and ideal beauty and wit. You may not feel too much like talking about your delicious dreams and fantastic fantasies, but you'll be surprised at just how much you will be able to communicate of these vague and elusive insights when you try. Find someone you trust and have a heart-to-heart, as you'll find it's a real joy to share your inner vision.

MONDAY, 19th. It's your most private and personal world of the imagination and dreams that sparkles with a burst of new energy from the powerful New Moon today, giving you the opportunity to put your inner life in perspective and order. This is your chance to withdraw from the hubbub of the world to contemplate your ideas and inspirations, as renovation, renewal and refreshing restoration spring gently up from your fevered subsconscious, ready to make you a peaceful, fulfilled and contented Lion!

TUESDAY, 20th. There are few things a tender pussycat likes more than a perfectly pleasant day surrounded by civilised and sophisticated companions, and that's what's on today's astral agenda. This is no time to hide away from the world, as it is through your social contacts with others that you'll derive most benefit from today's happy and harmonious heavens. Maybe an evening out with the gang or a visit to your local pub or club will fit the bill?

WEDNESDAY, 21st. Words have been uttered in the heat of the moment that hurt you more than you realised at the time, but now you've had time to reflect you'll be feeling blue. Don't let wounded pride prevent you from talking things over with your partner, for only through communicating your worst fears and anxieties can you begin to devise a practical and workable solution. A difficult, discouraging day, demanding plenty of patience.

THURSDAY, 22nd. In contrast to yesterday's sombre start, what a little ray of sunshine you are! I must wish you a happy solar return, for today the scintillating Sun swans back home to your own sign. There's no need to describe just how marvellous the weeks ahead will be, but to give you a wee taster, it's a period when you belt out a million kilowatts of confidence and creative brilliance. What a dazzler!

FRIDAY, 23rd. Domestic dramas and irrevocable changes affecting your home life lately may have taken their toll of your cash reserves and caused you a few anxious economic moments. Review the family finances today and you could be surprised to see just how far you've made your resources go. Encourage a candid conference amongst your kinfolk about the sensitive subject of loot and you'll all benefit from getting it off your chest.

SATURDAY, 24th. Your sixth sense tells you a loved one's tense and troubled Saturday. Even if all seems well on the surface, take the time to probe gently into any personal problems, as you'll intuitively know when to draw the line and respect their privacy. Chances are they'll appreciate your concern and jump at the chance to unburden themselves to you. What a sweet, sympathetic soul you are!

SUNDAY, 25th. You've been valiantly trying to keep your thoughts in some sort of order, and finally the heavens come to your assistance as Mercury returns to his senses and moves direct once more. It could take a wee while for you to untangle some of the crossed wires that have accumulated over the past weeks, so take things one step at a time and don't assume everything's resolved with just a few phone calls or letters.

MONDAY, 26th. Have you been neglecting your kith and kin lately? Whether it's your grey-haired mum or a long-lost cousin you promised to visit, now's the time to set your conscience to rest and fulfil all of your familial duties. You may be surprised at just how pleased they are to see you, and it'll give you a glorious chance to boast about your adventures and exploits. Even if it's just a quick phone call to your old dad, you'll be glad you made the effort.

TUESDAY, 27th. Home-loving Lions detest domestic discord and will do anything to keep the peace, but that's quite a challenge Tuesday as your partners seem to resent your devotion to domestic duty. You need to walk a tightrope between the demands of home and parents and those of your partners in life, whether business or romantic, and this leaves you exasperated and discouraged. Try not to let the pressures get to you – the chances are that the problems are very superficial and can be dealt with at an easier time.

WEDNESDAY, 28th. Cast aside the cares of the workaday week, for Wednesday's astral array is filled to the brim with bonhomie, benevolence and brilliance. Surround yourself with folk who know how to make you smile and you'll sail through the day in a good-humoured and happy mood, ready to cheer up any sad or sorrowful soul you meet. A message from far away gladdens your heart.

THURSDAY, 29th. Moderation was never your strong point, but if you don't temper your excitable impulses with a little tact and discretion today you may end up alienating the very people you've been so carefully cultivating over the past few days. Keep your cool when costing a creative project and look for a compromise to any problems rather than trying simply to impose your will on a reluctant backer. Not a good day for a gamble.

FRIDAY, 30th. Togetherness comes in the unexciting form of practical good sense and excellent organisation now. Get together with a partner you know has their feet firmly on the ground and look at logical ways of making the most of your shared time and talents. Paying attention to the pedantic details is what makes all the difference between success and failure as a team.

SATURDAY, 31st. There's just so much you can cram into a week and I think you've come close to the limits lately, so call a halt before your extra exertions undermine your health and tear your poor nerves to ribbons! You're inclined to be in a delicate state this Saturday and need plenty of peace and quiet to restore your batteries. Maybe a wee stroll in the country would help restore your normally rocklike stability? Take it easy, Leo!

AUGUST

SUNDAY, 1st. Peace at all costs for you, my dear. You're not interested in the slings and arrows of discontent that are being hurled at you from all quarters and in fact you want to retreat from the rigours of everyday life and take a welcome break. Holidays or outings taken away from the tourist traps will be very worthwhile. A new love could enter your life, but secretly!

MONDAY, 2nd. The Aquarian Full Moon is shining bright and clear on your horoscopic house of partnerships, giving you a celestial signal that it's time to get to work clearing out any cobwebs in your relationships with your nearest and dearest. A little ruthlessness now could save you a lot of bother in the future, so set any partnership problems to rights. There's no sense in trying to avoid the issue.

TUESDAY, 3rd. If the postman doesn't bring a good-humoured grin to your face with his offering today, make sure you meet and greet as many people as possible on this potentially thrilling Tuesday. Almost anyone you bump into now could give you just the idea you need to put your most ardent ambitions into action. Get into the swim and current affairs will soon sweep you on to success!

WEDNESDAY, 4th. Put your hard-headed act behind you, for this week you're interested only in enjoying the affectionate and indulgent delights on offer in the privacy of your own home. If you've a passionate partner to help you unwind so much the better, but you're equally content to drift along in a delicious daydream or lose yourself in a rapturous romantic movie. Put your feet up and forget all about your problems!

THURSDAY, 5th. Are you feeling stifled and bored with your world? Well, Thursday has the starry answer you need and you'll be surprised to discover that it doesn't involve anything more daring than a few hours spent in the stimulating company of your kith and kin. Get in touch with the clan, either by phone or through dropping in for a cuppa with a nearby relative. A wistful wander down Memory Lane with someone who shares your recollections will soon take you out of yourself.

FRIDAY, 6th. You'll get quite incensed and irate if you engage in talks about your beliefs and ideals this Friday, for you tend to take any hint of disagreement or contradiction as a personal insult, but are you sure that's the way to win folk round to your point of view? Courtesy costs nothing and will pay rich dividends in helping you to get your ideas across without embarking on a major dispute.

SATURDAY, 7th. A fully refreshing weekend is in store and you're raring to go once more, and even feel ready to take on a few extra challenges. You're especially keen to learn much more about this wide wonderful world, for you've a hankering for the far horizons. If you're very lucky, maybe you can jet off to the sunshine, but for most Leos it's the adventurous delights of a good book or travellers' tales that must provide the extra scope in your life.

SUNDAY, 8th. You fume and fulminate when you get wisecracks or superficial replies to your deep and profound questions this Sunday. Why can't folk give you a straight answer? The problem's rooted in your search for honesty and that's met with evasive prevarication. When doors are slammed shut and you're not made privy to secret discussions, sparks are sure to fly.

MONDAY, 9th. A delicate and charming day for you, when your usual impatience and blunt energy can be deliciously modified by a sensitive, sweet-natured and sympathetic outlook. You will find you can get along so much easier with the most difficult people, whether they're at work or simply in the street, so why not relax and enjoy this rare oasis of peace and harmony?

TUESDAY, 10th. Marvellous Mercury's march into your Sun sign from Tuesday will bring out the very articulate and expressive side of your powerful personality. It's the start of a busy, busy, busy period, so don't let opportunity slip by when it comes to communicating, chatting and getting connected with the right people. Not a phase to play the hermit as solitary activities of any kind will leave you high and dry! Go out into the world, ring a pal and socialise!

WEDNESDAY, 11th. Stand firm whilst all around you are wilting with the midweek blues and you'll make a mighty favourable impression on the powers that be, for they'll realise you have sterling qualities of drive and determination that'll take you far. This is a fine time to push your claim for an increase in pay, extra allowances or greater recognition, so don't hide your light under a bushel!

THURSDAY, 12th. Energetic wee Mars jogs joyfully into your horoscope's house of travel and communications, bringing a burst of activity that will have you trotting hither and thither carrying messages and running errands. It's a powerful period for getting your opinions and notions across to folk who've been missing the point, so don't waste a moment – circulate and communicate!

FRIDAY, 13th. Forget old wives' tales about the significance of this ill-omened date, for this is an excellent time to pull a few strings. You have some rather impressive acquaintances in your address book, or at least someone you know will have an influential friend or two. Don't be bashful when it comes to exploiting contacts –

maybe you've something to offer in exchange? Your Friday stars favour mundane matters and materialistic concerns.

SATURDAY, 14th. You can't open your mouth without putting your foot in it today, as you blurt out confidential information and let slip a secret entrusted to you. Steer well clear of controversial subjects as you chat to folk you meet now, keep the conversation light and inconsequential and you may avoid saying something you'll regret. Concentrate on the road when travelling, as you're apt to daydream.

SUNDAY, 15th. You're still super-sensitive to every undercurrent around you, especially as it affects your family. Relatives with a few personal problems will relish your kindly and compassionate approach and may well want to unburden themselves. It makes fascinating hearing to discover about all these skeletons in family closets!

MONDAY, 16th. If energy, intelligence and dynamic drive are called for, you can supply them in abundance on this busy, lively and active day. You're in no mood to take no for an answer and can usually find a way to talk folk round to your point of view without putting their backs up. Your personality is radiant and you blind all, young and old, with your savoir-faire and your debonair and suave appearance as well as your sparkling wit and incisive intelligence! This is a day to shine, so get out there and dazzle them!

TUESDAY, 17th. A fresh chapter in your book of life begins from today as the New Moon combines with Mercury in your own Sun sign, urging you to fling wide the door to a brand-new personal opportunity. You understand so well now that in order to progress you must leave the remnants of the past behind and strike out on a new path, guided only by your own intentions and understanding. New beginnings beckon!

WEDNESDAY, 18th. There's no holding you impulsive Leos back when you get a bee in your bonnet and thankfully there's no need to try, as you're on the right path and heading towards the winning post! Neighbours and siblings will be a wonderful source of inspiration and just plain brilliance, so make sure you pause just long enough to take their enthusiastic support on board!

THURSDAY, 19th. If your working world hasn't exactly been coming up to your exacting standards recently, hold on to something solid, because there are happenings akin to an astral earthquake on today's agenda. A truly miraculous set of events is presaged by the link-up of the erratic planet Uranus and the inspired rays of Neptune. Yawning Leos who are fed up with the mundane way that things are done will be awoken by just the right stimulus to get your pulse racing. The flair and originality that you can provide is what's needed now, so cast aside old ideas and work practices and show the world what you can really do!

FRIDAY, 20th. As the long-term processes of slow and subtle change continue throughout the year, today brings a celestial spotlight to remind you of what's going on. You may feel at times that your world is slowly falling apart around you, as the Neptune–Uranus link and Saturn battle for supremacy, but remember that the gulf between you and the folk you love is mostly in your own mind. Don't let a romantic situation sap your confidence – you'll be looking on the dark side and forgetting how bright things can be.

SATURDAY, 21st. If you've a colleague or a relative who thinks it's their duty to tell you just where you've been going wrong, they'll get short shrift from you Saturday. On the other hand, if you retire from the field of combat and bury your head in books or look forward to the prospect of travel, either for business or pleasure, you couldn't be better occupied. An ace day for a serious and intense approach to knowledge and learning.

SUNDAY, 22nd. After Saturday's titanic tussle your Sunday stars seem all sweetness and light, so make the most of an enjoyable opportunity to immerse yourself in the inconsequential trivia of life. Now the garden's beginning to blossom forth, perhaps you could potter around and sow a few seeds? A chat with someone who has years of experience will put you wise on a few pointers and help to pass a very pleasant few minutes.

MONDAY, 23rd. With the splendid support of the magnificent Sun from your solar house of monetary matters and inner values from today, you'll be able to set to rights any material mix-ups in your world. Take powerful and persistent action to penetrate right into the heart of any problem, whether it's cash starvation or a failure of feeling, and you'll set yourself up for a much more enriching and rewarding future.

TUESDAY, 24th. You're in the mood to stave off the Tuesday morning blues with a few little luxuries that'll dig altogether too deeply into your weekly allowance if you're not careful. Don't try to buy off a child or a youngster who's proving awkward with cash inducements or bribes, for you'll regret it in the long run as their demands increase whilst their behaviour worsens. Take a tough line now.

WEDNESDAY, 25th. A snippet of news that reaches you via a roundabout route could prove to be a real stroke of luck, as it gives you just the inside information you need to make some sense of an ambitious plan that's been proposed. This may not be the right time to go the whole hog and risk all to win all, but a minor wager, whether it's with time or money, should work out in your favour.

THURSDAY, 26th. If you're making too many demands on your bank balance you could be making trouble for yourself as you're an impatient and impetuously extravagant Lion now and hate to take no for an answer. If financial problems have built up you have the sharp wit and keen intellect to cut through a war of words and sort out for yourself an approach to your accounts that will smooth your fiscal path.

FRIDAY, 27th. Who's the blue-eyed boy or girl of the zodiac then? You've guessed, it's you! Voluptuous Venus, the heavenly body who chivvies up our love life, helps business affairs to prosper and endows us with a desire to look and be lovely, dances into your Sun sign from today. Treat yourself to a new outfit or a smart new hairdo as your cash increases along with your allure.

SATURDAY, 28th. Cast a critical eye over the fittings and fitments of your abode Saturday. If your home habitat doesn't match up to your luxurious Leonine standards, there's no reason to put up with it any longer. Make a detailed analysis of all you'd like to improve, including feasibility studies for your various options, and then you'll be in a powerful position to make your propositions to your family.

SUNDAY, 29th. You're a real soft touch this Sunday as the totally feminine influences of the Moon, combined with Venus, bring out your loving, sympathetic and caring side. If you're married, this is a marvellous time to let your other half know just how much you care, but watch out for folk who sense your vulnerable emotions and try to take advantage of you. Your resistance to any emotional appeal is zero now.

MONDAY, 30th. Income, investments and acquisitions are the chief talking point now, or at least they certainly should be. When it comes to material matters you're a sheer genius, able to see your way clear to making a positive profit out of even the most sterile and stagnant situation. A perfect day for dealing with your bank manager, stockbroker or insurance salesman.

TUESDAY, 31st. Changes made yesterday seemed a good idea at the time but now you could well be suffering the aftereffects as you confront the flood of fears and doubts about the wisdom of your actions. Don't take your anxious and apprehensive reactions too much to heart, as it's a momentary mood that'll soon pass once you allow yourself to look on the bright side once more. A glum and gloomy day if you give in to your melancholy mood.

SEPTEMBER

WEDNESDAY, 1st. An intense emotional experience will bring to the surface many complex behaviour patterns or deep psychological blockages. The mysterious magic of today's Full Moon evokes emotions from the depths, making you a susceptible and vulnerasble soul. While you're in touch with feelings and fears you normally keep hidden, take the opportunity to have a spring-clean in the cupboards of your inner being, eliminating any desires and compulsions that no longer have any place in your life.

THURSDAY, 2nd. Something a relative lets slip in an unguarded moment this Thursday will arouse your suspicions, as you're convinced something's afoot. Don't instantly assume they're up to no good, as there's really no reason to think badly of them. Make a few very discreet and diplomatic enquiries amongst your kith and kin and you could uncover a pleasant plot aimed at supplying you and your folks with a little extra income or a surprise party.

FRIDAY, 3rd. If you decided to flee far from the rat race today, you'll be up to your eyes in sheer enjoyment by now as you discover the many pleasures afforded by a break from routine. A holiday romance could bring a sparkle to your eye, too! If you're stuck with the same old surroundings, why not let your imagination roam free by dipping into a daring book or watching a film full of fantasy and frolics.

SATURDAY, 4th. You'll get quite hot under the collar if you engage in a discussion about topics close to your heart today, for you tend to take a theoretical disagreement to your views as a personal insult, which doesn't allow for much in the way of polite and polished debate. Don't forget your manners just because there are folk with diametrically opposite opinions. After all, it takes all sorts! Don't take risks when travelling now.

SUNDAY, 5th. Speak up, Leo! Blow your own trumpet loud and clear this Sunday and make absolutely sure your ambitious aims have been understood by all and sundry, for publicity's the key to total success today. An off-the-cuff journey may introduce you to brand-new people and places with tremendous personal potential for your own individual desires. Your actions are all blessed by a bountiful and benevolent bevy of planets now.

MONDAY, 6th. Even if the late summer sunshine is obscured by clouds, this is a fine time to potter around your garden, go for a restful walk in the country or take a trip to the seaside to breathe in some of that fabulous fresh air! City Lions will benefit from a brief visit to a local park or anywhere that'll allow you to get out of the house and away from the claustrophobic feel of four walls.

TUESDAY, 7th. Reactionary folk who find your recent innovations a mite threatening will weigh in with dire and dreadful warnings, trying to put you off your sensational stroke. If you're wise you'll listen respectfully and then carry on doing precisely what you planned in the first place. Certain practical points raised by gloomy folk may be valid but there's no need to take their entire pessimistic outlook on board.

WEDNESDAY, 8th. What a superbly serene Wednesday! You're at your most sensitive and sympathetic, wanting nothing better than to spend time with fond friends and doing a good turn to aid the love of your life. Your more self-centred ways are forgotten as you look around for ways of helping the folk who mean so much to you. You may not have much energy for socialising, but a low-key chat or informal outing will bring heaps of happiness.

THURSDAY, 9th. A pal who calls you penny-pinching may not be such a good friend after all – you can't help wondering if cash is all that interests them. That may not be very charitable but you're sick and tired of them harping on about their financial difficulties while pointedly commenting on your own relative affluence. Don't let them make you feel guilty just because you're not as fiscally foolish as them!

FRIDAY, 10th. Mighty Mars tangles with revolutionary Uranus and the battle call is heard loud and clear in your world. You're ready to defend your own ideas to the death rather than give way, and you could find that your attitude is like a red rag to a bull for the folk around. Stand up for your rights, but do try to be just a little more diplomatic and a lot less stubborn and uncompromising!

SATURDAY, 11th. A fine start to the weekend as far as your relationships are concerned. It would be a great idea to do something together with your other half, or at least in the company of folk you *both* know and love. Some good news comes through but check out its authenticity and accuracy before you start yelling alleluia.

SUNDAY, 12th. However hard you try to speak your mind, your tongue keeps tripping you up, you find you've a mind like a sieve or your brain just isn't in gear. You're somewhat sensitive to criticism and take things very personally, so perhaps you'd be better off using your imagination in a quiet, artistic pursuit rather than trying to make any insensitive folk understand your innermost feelings and subconscious thoughts. A Sunday for solitude.

MONDAY, 13th. Through being conscientious, careful and uncompromising now you could consolidate your entire pecuniary position. If you have richer relatives who haven't so far contributed as much as they might, lay a properly worked-out plan before them and point out the mutual benefits of working together to improve the family fortunes. There's nothing to be ashamed of in owning up to economic realities and doing what you can to bring about a brighter budgetary future for all. Don't be deflected from your perspicacious pecuniary plans.

TUESDAY, 14th. You may think that you can pull the wool over the eyes of your other half by concocting a flattering but totally false story to cover some of your recent actions, but you're the only one who's under any illusions today. Tall tales of any kind will only entangle you further in a Neptunian net of doubt and dismay, so stick religiously to the straight and narrow. Taking the line of least resistance in partnership affairs won't help in the long run.

WEDNESDAY, 15th. Though you're still caught up in the midweek round of duties and mundane tasks, the heavenly forces of the Moon and Neptune conspire to take you on a mystical journey far from the practical concerns you've been used to. You are in a dreamy, inspired frame of mind, busy formulating your ideas and ideals. A deep love of humanity and the beauties of nature is expressed in your every word and gesture. The only trouble is, the more boring everyday world hasn't gone away. Monetary matters especially demand your attention, so do what you have to do before your astral ascent into the realms of the spiritual.

THURSDAY, 16th. Today's New Moon in Virgo signals a fresh fiscal beginning for all Leos. Whether you're a rich Lion or down on your uppers, now's the perfect time to embark on a brand-new economic enterprise designed to improve your income. Don't try to tackle a complex cash situation on your own when a few words with a well-informed member of the family will help to put you on the right track.

FRIDAY, 17th. A superabundance of optimism is right up your street today. As far as you are concerned, nothing can go wrong, because your luck's in and the stars are smiling on your worldly fortunes. Hang on a minute – things may be fine now, but you must appreciate that there is a tomorrow, and where's your planning for that? Some affairs have to be settled now and that means investments, insurance policies and share interests. Turn your positivity to those ends and you will be totally justified in your bright views of the future. Though your luck is indeed good, it isn't wise to stretch it too far.

SATURDAY, 18th. It's a most enlightening Saturday for Leos who favour artistic and cultural excellence. You appreciate the beauties of anything, from a marvellous piece of classical music to magnificent modern works of art, for you're intellectually attuned to all that's harmonious in the world now. A chat with someone well-informed on matters of taste will bring much pleasure and add to your education.

SUNDAY, 19th. The domestic theme still dominates the heavens, so maybe you should take the opportunity of a day of rest to prowl around your abode looking for nooks and crannies that are crying out for improvement? Tot up a few of your ideas with the estimated cost and even if it seems beyond your current means, at least you'll know what kind of investment you're talking about. A chat with your kith and kin will help you to crystallise your ideas.

MONDAY, 20th. For once you're quite content to take the phone off the hook and put up the 'do not disturb' notice, as you could so easily ignore the realities of the Monday morning blues. Basically, you're a domesticated pussycat and want to spend time with your family, looking after your abode. It's a marvellous time finally to catch up with the ironing or (more to your taste!) the family gossip. A home-loving day.

TUESDAY, 21st. Your financial standing could be better and this is your chance to give it a bounteous boost. It doesn't matter if you've only a few bob to your name, for if you remember to look after the pennies the pounds will take care of themselves. In the light of this, delve into investment, pension or insurance plans and you could be hatching a nice little nest egg later.

WEDNESDAY, 22nd. You may have been told as a nipper that money was made for spending but there's no need to stick rigidly to that attitude! You're tempted by the good things of life today and just want to surround yourself by those luxuries that you deserve, but you could be forgetting the economic facts of life. So take it easy, for a little prudence with your cash won't go amiss now.

THURSDAY, 23rd. Your colossal creative capacity, coupled with your willingness to learn, will be the formula for success that you've been waiting for. Bombard people with letters, telephone calls and applications, and remember that there's no rest for the wicked and the Sun shines upon the righteous! Your communications flow with all the ease of well-oiled clockwork, so keep yourself wound up and on the go and you won't miss a trick.

FRIDAY, 24th. You can't bear the thought of doing the same old things every Friday and need to introduce a little entertainment and adventure into the more mundane areas of your world. Forget the upcoming weekend chores just for once and take off on an exploration of your neighbourhood, or further afield if you can. You'll be much happier as a result.

SATURDAY, 25th. The weekend has barely started, yet an insignificant detail like that won't hold you back when it comes to leisure and pleasure. You're in fine sociable form and just raring to make the most of the many enjoyable, entertaining and amusing opportunities for having a good time that are about to come your way. A get-together with neighbours could be a bundle of laughs, so don't turn down any invites, however casual.

132

SUNDAY, 26th. You're as jolly and jovial as can be Sunday, putting you in great demand in your social circle. Don't neglect your other half just because others are clamouring for your attention, for a few moments' quiet conversation with your loved one will yield rich rewards in terms of encouragement, assistance and aid in the future. You're rushed off your feet now with invitations, so live it up!

MONDAY, 27th. The energy that flows in your domestic sphere must be used positively and channelled into useful areas, otherwise you'll end up so seething and frustrated that you won't be able to make headway with plans you've been intending to tie up. A gent in the home is in for a spot of ego-bashing, so watch out for belligerent and bellicose action in the family.

TUESDAY, 28th. If fiscal affairs have been up and down like a roller-coaster ride recently, today's stars show a turnabout as the unconventional planet Uranus gets back on course, taking your monetary matters with him. A little stability will return to your pecuniary realities from today as events take an unexpected turn and you come up smelling of roses. Worries you've had about your financial future will look far less burdensome now. Perhaps a new and original approach to mortgages, investments or even arrears could turn a loss into a profit.

WEDNESDAY, 29th. Some of the decisions you've made recently concerning your entire emotional and economic foundation in life may seem a bit too drastic to tell your family all at once, but aren't you underestimating their resilience? Far from going off at the deep end and lecturing you on the need for common sense, they're likely to understand perfectly and offer a few wise and encouraging words of advice into the bargain. Open up to someone you can trust and you won't regret it.

THURSDAY, 30th. Energies of all kinds are running very high and mighty, making you feel like the proverbial cat on a hot tin roof. You want to do and experience so much that you could end up sitting still and dithering until the cows come home about what to do first, so take the opportunity of this lovely Full Moon to get your priorities in order and decide what projects are worth pushing ahead with.

OCTOBER

FRIDAY, 1st. From this first day of the new month your thoughts take a domestic turn as you consider your home life and ways in which to improve it. Organise a gathering of the clan this month, arrange an armistice if problems have popped up and voice your innermost feelings. It's a time of remembrance, so wander down Memory Lane with old photo albums and keepsakes and gently mull over the past.

SATURDAY, 2nd. You can be such a single-minded Lion when it comes to your headlong rush up the career ladder. But are you paying just a little too much attention to your professional aims and not enough to those nearer home who need your help and support? Someone in the family has been trying to catch your eye for ages, just to grab a couple of minutes of your priceless time. Look around you, Leo, the trust and affection you are surrounded with in your little tribe is at risk. Take the phone off the hook and have a heart-to-heart now. You may not solve all the problems, but you will show that you care.

SUNDAY, 3rd. You're fitted with a very short fuse by nature and everything on this unsettled Sunday seems ready to provide the spark required to set you off. It may be irritating relatives who make you see red over a disputed domestic issue or a bloody-minded boss who seems determined to beat you into submission, but either way you'll have a hard time keeping a civil tongue in your head. Try to avoid confrontation, for you're far from calm now.

MONDAY, 4th. Professionally you're not content to be a bystander or to be cast in a mere supporting role. You're after the perch right at the top of the tree and you'll be full of bright ideas about how to get there. If some of your schemes seem a little off-beat and unusual so much the better, as it's as well to show an individual and independent talent rather than following in the footsteps of lesser folk. You're a unique winner now!

TUESDAY, 5th. Sharp-tongued and short-tempered is the only way to describe the heavenly host this Tuesday. With such a forceful focus on sizzling energy in your horoscopic house of the home, you'll be ready to take on all comers at the smallest challenge to your ideas and opinions. What's more, there won't be many that can defeat your rapierlike wit now! Before you start to brandish your formidable verbal weapons, make sure that your position really is worth defending or you'll create unnecessary enmity within the confines of your little tribe.

WEDNESDAY, 6th. The future beckons with a benign and benevolent face today as jolly Jupiter holds out the promise of a world full of love, laughter and happiness. Generous, warm-hearted and optimistic, you're a joy to be with. Friends flock to your side and admirers in their thousands can't get enough of you – socially, you're a right little swinger, full of personality-plus and top of the popularity pops!

THURSDAY, 7th. Now's your golden galactic opportunity to find out just what's been giving your partner in life such a sour and unfriendly expression. Don't expect effusive affection, since it'll take a while for you to go through the details of any problems. A sagacious pal with experience of these situations will provide just the discreet support you need.

FRIDAY, 8th. The more you investigate your inner world, the more intrigued you are by the fascinating nooks and crannies that lie within. Don't get so drawn into the pleasure of contemplating your own navel that you disregard the more wordly delights on offer this weekend, for you might miss out on a chance to make the acquaintance of someone who could become a very good friend and neighbour.

SATURDAY, 9th. If your partner in life is listless and irritable today, don't be too surprised, as sombre Saturn makes a rare aspect to the great transformer, Pluto. Home life and domestic issues are at the root of this. Your mate will want some far-reaching changes made, and made now! This has all the signs of turning into a crisis if you aren't prepared to compromise. The important thing is to talk all issues over as calmly and rationally as you can. An airing of problems leads to an easing of the tense atmosphere, so don't be tempted to sweep anything under the carpet at a time when so much can be resolved.

SUNDAY, 10th. You'll earn for yourself a reputation as a real blabbermouth if you're not careful, as Sunday's stars also tend to loosen your tongue. Rather than spread a rumour or sow the seeds of suspicion, why not talk directly to the people involved in an issue that's worrying you? Family affairs will require careful handling, for some very excitable emotions lie just beneath the surface.

MONDAY, 11th. Your nearest and dearest have certain opinions and attitudes that just strike you as totally misguided and even mischievous or malicious. Try as you might, you can't hope to change their mind under such an obstinate, intransigent and implacable sky, but before you accuse other folk of being bloody-minded, shouldn't you own up to being just a tiny bit inflexible yourself? A difficult day, demanding tons of tact.

TUESDAY, 12th. In contrast to yesterday's troublesome skies, mighty Jupiter lights up the end of the tunnel in a most satisfying way Tuesday. Though the going may be slow, it is sure, and the prospect of a deeper understanding in your close relationships is a certainty. Your dealings with your partner in life, siblings and colleagues will be much closer now as your minds meet and a steady flow of communication ensues.

WEDNESDAY, 13th. What did I tell you? By opening your eyes to the generosity and goodwill that surrounds you, the whole pecuniary prospect of your world has brightened up no end. Why not show the love of your life how much you appreciate their loyal support and affectionate encouragement by buying them a wee gift? All it takes to please them profoundly is a small token of your love.

THURSDAY, 14th. Take care that you put your brain into gear before you speak out Thursday, for you're likely to rattle on, regardless of other folk's feelings. Your instincts are very vague today. All sorts of intuitions and inspirations may pop into your head from out of the blue, but you must rationally evaluate the meaning of the message before you act or pass it on.

FRIDAY, 15th. Yesterday's heavenly bustle continues to set your social world in a spiffing spin, but now your emotions and instincts are added to the astral equation. It's a splendid time to gather together with concerned neighbours to add lustre to your locale, whether it's community care or a new theatre group that's needed. Communicate and congregate now!

SATURDAY, 16th. That convivial and charming way you have with words will be your hottest property from Saturday. Over the coming weeks you will meet people or be put into situations where the way you express yourself and your ideas will be what sets you apart from your rivals. You're especially brilliant when it comes to handling females or artistic matters.

SUNDAY, 17th. The splendid Sun is ably supported and strengthened by strict Saturn on Sunday, giving the sensitive Lions of this world an open invitation to deal with practical affairs in a supremely sensible way. You have an abundance of energy and can channel it in the most efficient and effective ways that will ensure you achieve your aspirations. Partners offer sage advice that will put you on the right track.

MONDAY, 18th. You're a positive, forward-looking Lion at the best of times, but with the glorious rays of the Sun boosted by that other celestial giant, Jupiter, there's absolutely nothing that can stop you now! You will want to expand the range of your activities as well as your understanding and contacts with others today, and any moves you make to do this will be crowned with good fortune and success. So don't hesitate, seize your chances with both hands!

TUESDAY, 19th. Domestic disputes appear to be the order of the day, for you want your own way and won't feel the least bit inclined to compromise with your long-suffering family. Can you blame them if they seem a trifle touchy themselves as you make demand after demand? Go on, give your kith and kin some slack! If you're occupied in a little DIY, take extra care with sharp tools and don't take safety for granted.

WEDNESDAY, 20th. You're such a bright spark! Prepare to be crowned the 'Brain of Britain' this Wednesday, for there's such a fertile flood of innovative, inventive and ingenious ideas pouring out of your mouth and forth from your pen. If that seems far from the truth, maybe you should listen to the unconventional advice of a non-conformist relative, for they'll surprise you with the practical potential of their ideas and you could be the one to reap the rewards!

THURSDAY, 21st. A bright and breezy day dawns in which to get a thousand and one things done with the minimum of fuss and the maximum speed. You can change work and day-to-day routines without any disturbance or disruption and generally pep up the pace of your everyday chores. Family concerns are also much more positive and pleasing than they have been.

FRIDAY, 22nd. A slightly stressful stellar scenario sets your nerves on edge today as your iron constitution begins to bend and buckle under the strain of modern life. You've had your fill of tiresome talk and tittle-tattle, so why not take the phone off the hook, put up a 'do not disturb' sign or simply take yourself off for a walk, far from the madding crowd? You need a spot of peace and quiet to restore your battered batteries!

SATURDAY, 23rd. The Sun moves at a tense angle to your own Sun sign, bringing an amount of tension, but also dynamism into your life. Certainly you cannot afford to rest on your laurels as far as domestic conditions are concerned, as I bet my bottom dollar that someone in the family could make your life a misery. This situation needs some swift, firm action before the disruption amongst your kith and kin gets any worse.

SUNDAY, 24th. As a Leo you usually love the luxurious life with never a ripple to disrupt your familiar round, but come Sunday you're filled with restlessness and the desire to do something different, especially where your home or work is concerned. Why not try out a new recipe, sample some foreign food or get to know a colleague better? There's a delicious rapport between you and a loved one – like minds, they say . . . !

MONDAY, 25th. Mercury's wandering ways are in astral evidence once again as he hurries off in the opposite direction for a wee detour. It's your home life that's most affected as muddles and misunderstandings accrue amongst your confused kinfolk. Make an effort to note down important dates, appointments and facts, for you just can't rely on mere memory at the moment. Until mid-November you must double-check all domestic arrangements.

TUESDAY, 26th. If your family fortunes have faltered, check over the facts and figures with an expert adviser and you'll uncover a legal loophole, economic oversight or tangled tax situation that's at the root of the problem. Take ruthless action to set any shared finances on a more sound and stable footing Tuesday and you'll do yourself and others a fiscal favour.

WEDNESDAY, 27th. You're a poor wee pussycat as Mercury and Saturn combine their rays to bring a day of discontent and discouragement. Whatever the situation, you'll be looking on the dark side, so delay important discussions and debates until you can make a more positive impression. Your mind is gloomily geared to concentrated and limited tasks, so work on practical details of domestic and professional projects rather than on broader themes.

THURSDAY, 28th. That slow-moving giant, Saturn, swings into direct motion again from today, showing that the problems in your close relationships are drawing to a close. You can breathe a sigh of relief as your point of view will be more readily taken on board and agreements are easier to reach. Nothing from planning a joint bank account to whose turn it is to do the dishes will be such a source of controversy.

FRIDAY, 29th. 'Born free' – that's the call of the heavens today as you shake off any restrictions and want to go walkabout! It's the wide-open spaces where you've room to breathe that appeal to you, allowing you to express yourself fully and completely. Get out and explore life, whether it means a trip to the library for a stimulating book or taking off for some exotic foreign spot, for you need to broaden your horizons somehow, some way!

SATURDAY, 30th. You've no celestial excuse not to take a long, hard look at your career and ambitions in life. If professionally you're disconsolate and dissatisfied with your progress or believe that you've outgrown your previous goals, now's the time to make stringent cuts and changes careerwise. Your ego is terribly sensitive to criticism these days, so don't take things too much to heart.

SUNDAY, 31st. Domestic developments that fill you with excited enthusiasm seem to have the opposite effect on your partner in life this Sunday as they seem determined to come up with objections to every single initiative you've proposed. It's intensely annoying and very frustrating, but ranting and raving will get you nowhere fast! Patiently point out the benefits of your ideas and they'll gradually come round to your point of view.

NOVEMBER

MONDAY, 1st. Sweet success smiles on you from on high so you can look forward to a week when all the anxieties that have recently plagued you are lifted from your shoulders. If your delicate nerves have been stretched to the limit, you can begin to relax and unwind with a little help from your friends as folk show their willingness to offer support. At last you can get through to your nearest and dearest and deal diplomatically with disputes. Peace and plenty reign once more!

TUESDAY, 2nd. To meditate and ponder is the best advice I can offer this Tuesday, for you're not as rested and free of worry as you would like. There's every possibility that you're making matters more complicated or neurotic than they really are, so try not to get too fanatical about your fraught and fragile feelings, as you could be making a mountain out of a molehill. Power games of the most subtle sort are a dangerous way to resolve problems, so keep resentments out in the open.

WEDNESDAY, 3rd. You may be reluctant to devote yourself to the prosaic tasks of an ordinary Wednesday, as you're convinced that there's a better way to deal with the tedious trivia of life. You may be right, but don't let that justify a sloppy and slapdash approach to your work, for if you lose your concentration you'll only have to backtrack on the job.

THURSDAY, 4th. You appear to be an unusually reserved and reticent Lion this Thursday, but that doesn't mean that you're under a cloud. It's just that your immediate actions and interests are all on a purely private and personal level concerned with propelling your kith and kin into a more powerful position. Confidential contracts to boost the family resources are favoured, so chat to the experts or organise a profitable investment plan now.

FRIDAY, 5th. For a laconic Leo you've been mighty loquacious and talkative lately and, quite honestly, you're all talked out! Peace and quiet is your chief craving this Friday as you conclude that silence is golden after all. Soothe your jangled nerves with a little mellow music or stroll in the open air to relish the sights and sounds of nature. You'll soon be back on an even keel.

SATURDAY, 6th. As you gaily gabble away to your cronies this sociably scintillating Saturday, you're in danger of opening your mouth a wee bit too wide and letting slip a few confidential facts and private opinions. You don't mean any harm, for we all know you wouldn't deliberately hurt a fly, but you'll need to weigh your words with a little extra care now if you're to avoid inadvertently causing offence.

SUNDAY, 7th. You can have too much of a good thing and that's the way you're beginning to feel Sunday as family feuds and domestic dramas begin to get on your nerves and make you itch for less stifling and sentimental interests. Try not to be too blatant in your desire to escape from the cosy clutches of your family, for their feelings are easily hurt and you don't really want to rock the boat. Or do you?

MONDAY, 8th. Even if you're feeling diffident and doubtful Monday you should put on a brave front and brazen it out with everyone you meet, for you'll be surprised at just how easy it is to convince folk that you know what you're talking about. If things get tricky as they ask you for details you don't have at your fingertips, turn the query aside with a joke and you'll soon find others rallying round to save your bacon. Luck is on your side now!

TUESDAY, 9th. Any creative schemes or ideas you've been sitting on should be put into practice Tuesday. Be down to earth with all your airy-fairy brainwaves and you'll soon have a bubbling enterprise and all the rewards that go with it. A productive period begins, so channel your energies effectively into the weeks ahead and you'll win all the acclaim your heart could desire. Amour enters a passionate phase!

WEDNESDAY, 10th. Domestic bliss is forecast as Jupiter, that genial bringer of jollity, moves into your horoscopic area of home, heritage and family feeling. A wonderful aura of harmony descends on your living arrangements, and family members will be more helpful and positive than they have been for ages. Many Leos will now be considering moving to a larger property or otherwise improving their immediate environment. A creative, artistic flair is also enhanced today, so the challenge of redesigning your living space is one you'll relish.

THURSDAY, 11th. That gentle giant of the zodiac, Jupiter, makes his imperial progress into your solar house of home and family, bringing a wonderful period of peace and contentment to all Leos. Jupiter does everything on a grand scale, so it's a good time to think of expanding things domestically, whether it's a bonny bouncing new addition in nappies or a move to a bigger property. Investments in land are well starred now.

FRIDAY, 12th. There's a total solar eclipse today, putting a powerful emphasis on all family affairs. If you're contemplating a move, now's the perfect time to make a fresh start in a brand-new area. If you're staying put, maybe you should consider a spot of rebuilding or redecorating totally to transform your abode, for 'out with the old and in with the new' is today's motto!

SATURDAY, 13th. Everyone, from your family to the lady who makes the office teas, is endowed with a fascinating quality that somehow makes the dullest of days different and exciting. Keep your eyes open for the individual little quirks that make each of us so unique and you'll be thrilled to discover what an extraordinary world you inhabit! Mind you, some of your views could cause a few raised eyebrows, but when did that ever worry you?

SUNDAY, 14th. You really set the cat amongst the pigeons yesterday with some of your comments about the way your home is organised, for you're faced now with some very fierce and fervent feelings from the family. The chances are they haven't fully understood what you're trying to achieve so don't just condemn them for being dull and dreary stick-in-the-muds. By understanding and appreciating their concerns you'll soon win them round to your point of view.

MONDAY, 15th. As such a home-loving Leo now, domestic disturbances will always catch you on the raw and you've certainly been through the mill since mid-October. Well, from Monday you can start licking your wounds when the atmosphere in your abode changes for the better. Patch up quarrels now and forgive and forget all those harsh words said in the heat of the moment.

TUESDAY, 16th. If you're responsible for a youngster's development or feel obliged to support your spouse in an ambitious enterprise, you're ready to make the most of Tuesday's sensible sky. Anything from meeting emotional needs to making sure they have enough clean socks will make all the difference in helping your loved ones lead effective lives. Behind every success story there's a proud Leo now!

WEDNESDAY, 17th. Workwise, Wednesday shows an uplift in your mood and enthusiasm. The mighty planetary pair, Uranus and Neptune, get together once more to provide a brilliant flash of inspiration, ending all feelings of being in a rut. Your mind is full of novel ideas concerning your mundane life, and boring duties can be transformed now into a deeply satisfying challenge that sets your pulse racing. If job satisfaction has been lacking, today should see a remarkable, unexpected upturn in your fortunes.

THURSDAY, 18th. You have an opulent opportunity Thursday to settle any long-standing domestic disputes or family feuds by insisting on a more open and honest attitude from all concerned. You'll set an exceptional example by your own willingness to own up to hidden hostility and by bedtime you'll find that you've totally transformed the atmosphere of your home base from one of tension to trust.

FRIDAY, 19th. There's such an explosive and argumentative planetary pairing in today's sky you'd be wise to take a little extra care, just to be on the safe side. The trouble comes from family members who seem to know just what to say to trigger your temper. A shouting match will get you nowhere, but it might relieve some fervent feelings! Be extra vigilant against accidents in the home.

SATURDAY, 20th. As you peer across the breakfast table at your other half you'll be dismayed to see a long face that looks as if its owner's bearing the weight of the entire world on their shoulders.

Pretty soon you'll be feeling glum and gloomy yourself if you don't take steps to snap out of it. It may be an uphill struggle at times, but if you put your mind to it you can turn a melancholy mood into a more cheerful humour. Don't take depressing notions too seriously, for you'll soon see the bright side.

SUNDAY, 21st. There's no peace for a Lothario-like Leo this week, it seems, for now it's the family's turn to find fault with your personal partnerships. It could be they're simply teasing you tenderly, so don't take too much offence and assume they're all out to get you. Learn to laugh about your own failings and foibles occasionally and you'll find life much easier!

MONDAY, 22nd. As soon as the Sun shines in Sagittarius, so you come out of the shadows feeling revitalised, restored and refreshed by your ruler's golden eye. This is a glorious period for creative achievement and displaying what you're capable of to the world at large. You want to enjoy life to the full and at the same time feel you're contributing to the human race and mankind as a whole. You're a powerhouse of activity and energy, Leo!

TUESDAY, 23rd. Sink thankfully back into the comforting and cosy lap of your family and set yourself up for a serene and soothing Tuesday. The ordinary, peaceful and straightforward things of life, such as pottering round the garden and cooking a proper meal, are what give you the greatest pleasure now, so indulge yourself and leave your extraordinary plans for another day.

WEDNESDAY, 24th. It seems this entire week is filled with fabulous fun, for even though it's not Christmas yet, you're clearly in the mood to start the celebrations a little early! Accept any social opportunities that come your way with open arms and, while you're at it, maybe you can issue a few invitations and arrange an impromptu shindig at your place? Don't restrict the revels to your own immediate circle, as this is a brilliant opportunity to include fascinating new folk in your life.

THURSDAY, 25th. The carefully nurtured harmony of your love life is disrupted and put into disarray by rebellious Uranus, giving you and your partner in life itchy feet and an unpredictable temper.

Inject a little inventiveness and individual freedom into your one-to-one affairs and you'll both be a lot happier. Expect the unexpected when travelling!

FRIDAY, 26th. You hate to admit it, even to yourself, but you do care deeply about your public image, and crave the respect and admiration of your peers just as much as the rest of us. You're extra-sensitive to the slings and arrows of Dame Fortune this Friday, so don't tackle anything too demanding or controversial. Your bold and brazen bravado will soon return, so why not give yourself a break?

SATURDAY, 27th. As you try to make your way in the world Saturday you'll find your mind wandering back to purely domestic concerns. Maybe there's a family feud to be mended or troubled kinfolk in need of support? Your mind's just not on external affairs, so keep your official schedule as light as possible and rush back to the cosy comforts of your own abode. Your first loyalty now must be to your private life.

SUNDAY, 28th. Some very firm family feelings are activated by Sunday's moody stars, and if you're not careful you'll trigger a tantrum that'll destroy the amiable atmosphere of your home. You're inclined to be intransigent and obstinate yourself if your career becomes the topic of conversation, so before you all end up at loggerheads, try some straight talking.

MONDAY, 29th. A brilliant chapter is about to begin in your world, embracing your creative potential, babies, love life and all those things that are nearest and dearest to your heart. But first things first, and you must begin to shut the door on any outdated material or situations that have prevented you from forging ahead.

TUESDAY, 30th. You've had your optimistic eyes on the pecuniary prize for long enough and now it's high time you worked out precisely what you and your partner want to accomplish with any good fortune coming your way. Get down to brass tacks and discuss the details involved in reaching the glittering summit of success.

DECEMBER

WEDNESDAY, 1st. You heave a sigh of heartfelt relief as you realise the weekend's almost arrived, for you've had enough of mundane demands and duties and yearn to sample the softer pleasures of life. Don't confine yourself to seeking a purely selfish source of satisfaction, as you'll enjoy yourself far more if you share your treats with someone you care for. Kindness is its own reward now.

THURSDAY, 2nd. The planet of love leaps into your solar house of creativity and social sparkle, making you ultra-attractive to everyone you meet. You're sure to be the centre of admiring attention wherever you show your bonny face now, so stock up on glamorous glad rags! When you're not partying the night away, display your inimitable talents in music and the arts.

FRIDAY, 3rd. Why wait for the weekend to whisk your sweetheart away for some sparkling conversation and some plush grub? Your Friday stars hold a welter of passionate pleasures, so it would be a shame to waste your chances by supping solo! Give your artistic tastes and talents a look-in, for your refined and cultivated appreciation of beauty is at its tiptop best today.

SATURDAY, 4th. Sensational Saturday stars serenade you, so give in to a little midwinter madness and step into a sparkling social spotlight! A romantic dinner *à deux*, dancing the night away by magical moonlight, or a fun-packed party of spirited and stimulating pals all give you your chance to shine. Don't pine away on your tod when companionship and amour await!

SUNDAY, 5th. Something said by a close neighbour or a relative on Sunday will have you simmering beneath the surface as your emotions are involved. You'll need to get any upset off your chest but do remember you're in the grip of a purely subjective response that may have no rational basis. Likewise, as you chat with your nearest and dearest, bear it in mind that they're apt to be just as sensitive.

MONDAY, 6th. It's been an expensive winter so far, what with one thing and another, and as far as you can see this Monday, the pecuniary pressures aren't about to let up, especially in the run-up to Christmas. Don't bury your head in the sand where your personal budget is concerned, even if your bank balance does make pretty grim reading. Maybe you can discuss the matter with family and friends and look for ways of cutting your costs? A little time spent now getting your economic act together will definitely deliver delightful dividends!

TUESDAY, 7th. It's all very well having opinions or ideas that show your creative prowess, but unless you do something to crystallise them or express them in a purely practical way, you could talk forever and a day and achieve very little. Action speaks louder than words, so don't delay in formulating plans or ventures that prove there's an enterprising entrepreneur buried inside you and dying to get out.

WEDNESDAY, 8th. All work and no play is no way of life for a luscious Lion, so make the most of Wednesday's wonderfully sociable stars. Romance the night away with someone very special, make for a midweek party with plenty of action or invite a few frolicsome friends round to your place for an evening's entertainment. With you as happy host, any occasion is sure to be a sparkling success!

THURSDAY, 9th. You can look back on your year with pride and pleasure, for you've achieved a great deal that's very much to your credit. Use your positive reflections as a basis for any resolutions you're contemplating, as there's no need to play small when you've such ample proof of your own excellent aptitudes and abilities. The words of a youngster will fill you with hope for a better future.

FRIDAY, 10th. This is a fine Friday for circulating amongst colleagues or inviting some fascinating folk back to your pad for anything from a casual chat to a high-powered discussion. You have plenty of positive ideas and can't wait to share them with the people whose opinions you most respect and admire. If you're a lone Lion, you could meet with a potential partner as you mix and mingle now.

SATURDAY, 11th. Your kith and kin see nothing but good coming from your actions and as a result egg you on to tackle ever greater professional challenges, but are you sure you're not biting off more than you can chew? Their faith in your abilities is very touching but you're the one who must face up to the harsh world of business and work in general. Strike a careful balance between optimism and sound sense.

SUNDAY, 12th. Your artistic aptitudes are honed to perfection now, so go for some ambitious objectives that show your talents off to the full. Everything, from the fine arts to photography or any kind of acting, dancing or drawing, will bring out your potential and also cause you deep spiritual satisfaction. A very romantic day when you've a passion for art, amour and enjoyment.

MONDAY, 13th. Births, pregnancies and anything relating to new life, indeed creation of any sort, are highlighted today. To be creative is often misunderstood – we assume it means to be a fine actor, brilliant artist or splendid singer, but that's only part of it; it's also having the ability to express your natural talents and ideas in the way only you can. That's something you must do now.

TUESDAY, 14th. Did you resolve to exercise every day this year, cut down on smoking, or treat yourself to a weekly sauna? By now you may be questioning the wisdom of your past overenthusiastic intentions, but rather than give up the idea completely and slide back to your bad old habits, give your body a break and look after it properly for once. You'll be surprised at how much support and encouragement you receive from your family. This is particularly important now as this can be quite a self-indulgent time of year. Don't struggle on alone when help is at hand!

WEDNESDAY, 15th. If you've been on edge lately, your health could be suffering somewhat and today's restless heavens will be bringing any ailments and complaints to the fore in an unexpected and startling way. Alternatives to the conventional health-care regimes will be worth considering as you're in an experimental mood and need to try something new.

THURSDAY, 16th. The glamorous world of romance is never far from a luscious Leo's mind and today the heavens are urging you to indulge in your taste for the delights of amour. Whether you want to paint the town red or snuggle up for a cosy twosome at home, you need congenial company to share your pleasures with now. Single Lions should soon be able to set the situation to rights.

FRIDAY, 17th. Someone you met yesterday will continue to occupy your thoughts in the nicest possible way! Married Lions have a golden opportunity to talk things over in the peace and quiet of a somnolent Friday, for communication is the key to happy and harmonious relationships. You may not have any earth-shattering news to impart but it makes such a difference simply to share the mundane events and problems of life.

SATURDAY, 18th. Preoccupied with the many personal pleasures lavished on you lately, you're apt to forget your partner in life and today if you don't take steps to share some of the excitement they'll remind you forcibly of the fact. Maybe you should whisk your spouse off for an evening out to make up for past neglect? If you're a lone Leo, someone in your social circle could catch your eye and set your pulse racing.

SUNDAY, 19th. You're a slightly strained and stressful Lion on Sunday as emotional pressures build up in an intimate relationship. Even if your sex life is perfectly peachy, there are conflicting demands pulling you this way and that, upsetting your equilibrium. Don't be too dismayed if you can't decide on your best course of action just yet. Why not simply bide your time and wait for the fog to clear?

MONDAY, 20th. Pioneering Mars pushes his way into your solar house of work and health from today and instigates an era of increased efficiency and effectiveness. You must be prepared to put in some hard and demanding work in the weeks ahead, for only by showing a spark of individual initiative will you progress on to the levels you deserve. You'll need to tread a tactful line between promoting yourself and maintaining amicable relations with workmates.

TUESDAY, 21st. The winter solstice is shining and the Sun dips to his nadir and leaves you pondering some of the essential issues of life. Nothing is more essential than your health, so don't allow yourself to neglect the wellbeing of your mind, body or spirit but do what you can to ensure physical and mental vitality for the coming festivities and the approaching New Year. Take good care of yourself, my dear!

WEDNESDAY, 22nd. You're such a raging Lion now as the Sun's golden rays are mixed with the blood-red glow of macho Mars. You'd better steer clear of touchy topics as you could be goaded into action and have no patience with folk who try to stand in your way. It's a great day to start a new project, whether it's a new physical regime or a new job, so long as you can work independently and energetically.

THURSDAY, 23rd. The splendid celestial situation is prompting you to surround yourself with some youthful folk as you'll be amazed at just how open their minds can be and you'll appreciate the vast vistas of understanding and enquiry they can suggest to you. A playful and relaxed approach to serious matters can yield valuable and interesting insights and intriguingly ingenious ideas.

FRIDAY, 24th. Voluptuous Venusian vibes combine rapturously with the lively light of madcap Mercury on this Christmas Eve, endowing you with pure, unadulterated superstar quality! If romance is the name of your particular game, you'll soon have a fervent flock of ardent admirers trailing you around and hanging breathlessly on your every word. Any artistic projects you've taken under your wing will blossom and bloom under your exquisite aesthetic insight. What a terrific Leo you are!

SATURDAY, 25th. What a terrific wee pussycat you are! Christmas Day's go-ahead sky goads you into self-assertive action that'll help you to take your world by storm. Even though this is a day of jollity and restful repose, you are raring to get something worthwhile done. It's your everyday activities that are injected with astral urgency as your patience with delays and obstacles finally runs out. You can get so much done in your energetic assault on the day's tasks, but don't put too much strain on your physical fitness.

SUNDAY, 26th. There's an amount of opposition to certain plans you want to put into practice this Boxing Day. It could be that you've a career to pursue that isn't compatible with your love life, or perhaps you're being too influenced by your other half and your ambitions are suffering. Find out what's good for you *and* your relationships.

MONDAY, 27th. Any hopes you may have for advancement in your career or an improvement in your working conditions should be mulled over in detail when you get a moment to yourself this Monday. It may still be a holiday for many, but there's much that you can do in terms of clarifying your own attitude to your everyday routine and thinking through the steps needed to make it more congenial. A chat with concerned relatives or neighbours may put you on the track of a better job.

TUESDAY, 28th. Perhaps because of an inner anxiety or a long-ignored guilt gnawing away at your subconscious, you just can't figure out what you feel today. It's time you came to terms with such vague, undefined and uneasy apprehensions, as today's Cancerian Full Moon endows you with the piercing insight required to sort out the purely imaginary from more pressing problems. Psychic sensitivity seeps into your consciousness now.

WEDNESDAY, 29th. You're in danger of losing your action-packed image this Wednesday as the Moon meanders moodily through your horoscopic house of reverie, reflection and restraint. I wouldn't worry though, for all of us need an occasional opportunity to switch off and recharge our inner batteries and you'll soon be back to your usual fighting form. A dreamy day, when all you want to do is stare into space and let your imagination run free.

THURSDAY, 30th. I know you love good food, but sometimes your eyes are just too big for your tummy and that could be the problem now if you're feeling peaky or off colour! There's no need to go to the other extreme and starve yourself into submission, but instead strike a happy medium and you'll soon be as fit as a fiddle again. Choose a sensible diet for the sake of your health. I should think it's time to reduce that waistline which has grown alarmingly over the Christmas break.

FRIDAY, 31st. A positive, pleasant and promising day dawns, so prepare to enjoy yourself to the full! Nothing spectacular is needed to keep you beaming with bliss, for the simplest of entertainments serves to keep you diverted and delighted. If you can spend a little time with some youngsters you'll feel encouraged and inspired by their innocent enjoyment of life, so don't stick to grown-up company when chatting with children can help keep you young. What could be a more fabulous start to a brand New Year?